AAT

AF621527

Level 4

Diploma for Professional Accounting Technicians

Advanced Business Awareness

Course Book

From September 2026

BPP LYCEUM EDUCATION GROUP

First edition 2026

ISBN 9781 0355 4445 5

ISBN (for internal use only) 9781 0355 4065 5

eISBN 9781 0355 4466 0

British Library Cataloguing-in-Publication Data

A catalogue record for this book is available from the British Library

Published by

BPP Learning Media Ltd
BPP House, Aldine Place
142–144 Uxbridge Road
London W12 8AA

learningmedia.bpp.com

Your learning materials are printed on paper obtained from traceable sustainable sources.

The contents of these learning materials are intended as a guide and not professional advice. Although every effort has been made to ensure that the contents of this book are correct at the time of going to press, BPP makes no warranty that the information in this book is accurate or complete and accept no liability for any loss or damage suffered by any person acting or refraining from acting as a result of the material in these learning materials.

Contents

Introduction

Introduction to the course iv

Skills bank vi

Introduction to the assessment vii

Key to icons viii

AAT qualifications ix

AAT Practice Assessment ix

Glossary of terms x

1 Understanding business decision making 1

2 Understanding organisational effectiveness 31

3 Understanding ethics and law in an accounting environment 57

4 Understanding the effective use of data in business 83

5 Understanding the importance of sustainability in business 117

Test your learning answers 145

Glossary 155

Bibliography 161

Index 165

Introduction to the course

Syllabus overview

This unit prepares students for real-world challenges and opportunities in the business environment, enhancing their employability and professional growth. By understanding complex business concepts and practices, students will be able to make informed decisions, improve organisational effectiveness, and contribute to sustainable business practices.

Students will learn how businesses set their goals and strategies, including the use of vision, mission statements, and objectives. They will understand how to make decisions that align with these goals and evaluate the impact of economic factors such as competition, economic growth, government policies, interest rates, inflation, international trade, supply and demand, and unemployment on business performance. This knowledge will enable students to make informed and strategic decisions that contribute to the success of their organisations.

Students will develop skills to improve personal effectiveness through effective time management and enhancing communication skills. They will learn the importance of collaboration, escalation, and delegation. Additionally, students will gain a deeper understanding of promoting equality, diversity, and inclusion (EDI) in the workplace and managing organisational changes effectively. These skills will help students become more efficient and adaptable professionals, capable of fostering a positive and inclusive work environment.

Students will learn the difference between laws and ethics and the importance of professional ethics in handling ethical conflicts and legal issues. They will gain skills to identify and address money laundering, bribery, and whistleblowing, and understand the legal protections for whistleblowers. This knowledge will help students navigate complex ethical and legal challenges in their professional roles, ensuring they act with integrity and uphold the highest standards of professional conduct.

Students will be equipped with the skills to collect, clean, and analyse data, understanding the principles of data protection and the importance of protecting commercially sensitive information. They will learn how a business can use data analytics to make better business decisions. This will enable students to leverage data to drive business performance and make informed decisions that enhance organisational efficiency and effectiveness. Students will also understand the issues arising in the use of social media and other digital platforms.

Students will understand key sustainability concepts and standards, including the United Nations Sustainable Development Goals (UN SDGs) and the importance of sustainability reporting under IFRSs. They will learn how to promote sustainable business practices and recognise the challenges and benefits of implementing sustainability policies. This knowledge will empower students to contribute to the development and implementation of sustainability strategies within their organisations, promoting long-term environmental, social, and economic sustainability.

Test specification for this unit assessment

Assessment method	Marking type	Duration of assessment
Computer based assessment	Wholly computer marked	2 hours 30 minutes

	Learning outcomes and objectives	Weighting
1	Understand business decision making	25%
2	Understand organisational effectiveness	15%
3	Understand ethics and law in an accounting environment	30%
4	Understand the effective use of data in business	10%

Learning outcomes and objectives		Weighting
5	Understand the importance of sustainability in business	20%
Total		**100%**

Assessment structure

- Duration: 2 hours 30 minutes
- Competency is 70%
- The total number of marks for this assessment is 80

Note. This is only a guideline as to what might come up, based on the AAT's sample. The format and content of each task may vary from what we have listed below.

Your assessment will consist of eight tasks.

The assessment will take the form of a computer-based test. The assessment will require computer marking and the results will be available instantly.

Task	Learning outcomes and objectives	Max marks	Chapter ref	Study complete
1	1.1 Organisational strategy and objectives	8	Chapter 1	
2	2.1 and 2.2 Personal effectiveness; Equity, diversity and inclusion (EDI)	8	Chapter 2	
3	1.2 Position analysis	8	Chapter 1	
4	4.1-4.3 Recording data; Using data and data protection; Presenting data	10	Chapter 4	
5	1.3, 2.1, 2.2, 4.1-4.3 Cost-benefit analysis; Personal effectiveness; Equity, diversity and inclusion (EDI); Recording data; Using data and data protection; Presenting data	12	Chapters 1, 2 and 4	
6	3.1 and 3.2 Ethics and professional scepticism; Law	10	Chapter 3	
7	5.1-5.3 Introduction to sustainability; Sustainability standards and reporting; Business sustainability	10	Chapter 5	

Task	Learning outcomes and objectives	Max marks	Chapter ref	Study complete
8	3.1, 3.2, 4.1-4.3, 5.1-5.3 Ethics and professional scepticism; Law; Recording data; Using data and data protection; Presenting data; Introduction to sustainability; Sustainability standards and reporting; Business sustainability	14	Chapters 3, 4 and 5	

Skills bank

Our experience of preparing students for this type of assessment suggests that to obtain competency, you will need to develop a number of key skills.

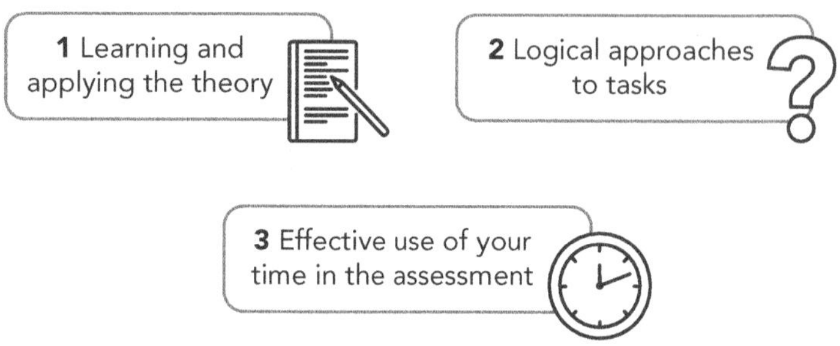

What do I need to know to do well in the assessment?

It requires good overall awareness of many parts of your AAT studies so far and should be seen as an ideal way of applying much of what you have already learnt as context for the new content that you will see, showing how audits are conducted in practice.

To be successful in the assessment you need to:

- Know the new material introduced in each chapter, having practised a number of tasks that reflect the real assessment.
- Apply the techniques demonstrated to 'real life' situations as presented in each task. These will often be tested using scenarios where you can consider what would really happen if you were the accountant.

Assumed knowledge

Advanced Business Awareness is one of the Level 4 units. You need to understand the Level 2 unit, *Business Environment*, and the Level 3 unit, *Business Awareness*, before taking this unit.

Assessment style

In the assessment you could complete tasks by:

(a) Entering narrative by selecting from drop down menus of narrative options known as **picklists**

(b) Using **drag and drop** menus to enter narrative

(c) Typing in numbers, known as **gapfill** entry

(d) Entering **ticks**

You must familiarise yourself with the style of the online questions and the AAT software before taking the assessment. As part of your revision, log in to the **AAT website** and attempt its **online practice assessments**, found within the 'Lifelong Learning Portal'.

Introduction to the assessment

The question practice you do will prepare you for the format of tasks you will see in the *Advanced Business Awareness* assessment. It is also useful to familiarise yourself with the introductory information you **may** be given at the start of the assessment. For example:

- This assessment contains **eight tasks** and you should attempt to complete **every** task.
- Each task is independent. You will not need to refer to your answers to previous tasks.
- The total number of marks for this assessment is **80**.
- Read every task carefully to make sure you understand what is required.
- Where the date is relevant, it is given in the task data.
- Both minus signs and brackets can be used to indicate negative numbers **unless** task instructions state otherwise.
- You must use a full stop to indicate a decimal point. For example, write 100.57 **not** 100,57 or 10057.
- You may use a comma to indicate a number in the thousands, but you don't have to. For example, 10000 and 10,000 are both acceptable.
- You will need to double click to enter values into a gapfill or cell within a table.

Once you have clicked 'Continue' you will not be able to return to this page. You will be able to view the 'Assessment information' in the references section at each task position.

(a) As you revise, use the **BPP Passcards** to consolidate your knowledge. They are a revision tool perfect for packing in that last-minute revision.

(b) Attempt as many tasks as possible in the **Exam Practice kit**. There are plenty of assessment-style tasks which are excellent preparation for the real assessment.

(c) Always **check** through your own answers as you will in the real assessment, before looking at the solutions in the back of the Exam Practice Kit.

Key to icons

Key term

A key definition which is important to be aware of for the assessment.

Formula to learn

A formula you will need to learn as it will not be provided in the assessment.

Formula provided

A formula which is provided within the assessment and generally available as a pop-up on screen.

Activity

An example which allows you to apply your knowledge to the technique covered in the Course Book. The solution is provided at the end of the chapter.

Illustration

A worked example which can be used to review and see how an assessment question could be answered.

Assessment focus point

A high priority point for the assessment.

Open book reference

Where use of an open book will be allowed for the assessment.

Real life examples

A practical real life scenario.

AAT qualifications

The material in this book may support the following AAT qualifications:

AAT Level 4 Diploma for Professional Accounting Technicians

Supplements

From time to time we may need to publish supplementary materials to one of our titles. This can be for a variety of reasons, from a small change in the AAT unit guidance to new legislation coming into effect between editions.

You should check our supplements page regularly for anything that may affect your learning materials. All supplements are available free of charge on our supplements page on our website at:

learningmedia.bpp.com/pages/resources-for-students

Improving material and removing errors

BPP Learning Media do everything possible to ensure the material is accurate and up to date when sending to print. In the event that any errors are found after the print date, they are uploaded to the following website:

learningmedia.bpp.com/pages/aat-errata

These learning materials are based on the qualification specification released by the AAT in November 2025.

AAT Practice Assessment

The AAT practice assessments mimic the real exam and so must be attempted prior to taking the real exam. You should attempt these using a laptop/desktop computer, as this will give you a better feel for the actual AAT exam conditions.

Please note, at the end of each test you will be presented with feedback which you should review.

Use this link below to access the assessment required:

https://www.aat.org.uk/learning-portal.

Glossary of terms

It is useful to be familiar with interchangeable terminology including IFRS and UK GAAP (generally accepted accounting principles).

Below is a short list of the most important terms you are likely to use or come across, together with their international and UK equivalents.

UK term	International term
Profit and loss account	Statement of profit or loss (or statement of profit or loss and other comprehensive income)
Turnover or Sales	Revenue or sales revenue
Operating profit	Profit from operations
Reducing balance depreciation	Diminishing balance depreciation
Depreciation/depreciation expense(s)	Depreciation charge(s)
Balance sheet	Statement of financial position
Fixed assets	Non-current assets
Net book value	Carrying amount
Tangible assets	Property, plant and equipment
Stocks	Inventories
Trade debtors or debtors	Trade receivables
Prepayments	Other receivables
Debtors and prepayments	Trade and other receivables
Cash at bank and in hand	Cash and cash equivalents
Long-term liabilities	Non-current liabilities
Trade creditors or creditors	Trade payables
Accruals	Other payables
Creditors and accruals	Trade and other payables
Capital and reserves	Equity (limited companies)
Profit and loss balance	Retained earnings
Cash flow statement	Statement of cash flow

Accountants often have a tendency to use several phrases to describe the same thing! Some of these are listed below:

Different terms for the same thing
Nominal ledger, main ledger or general ledger
Subsidiary ledgers, memorandum ledgers
Subsidiary (sales) ledger, sales ledger
Subsidiary (purchase) ledger, purchase ledger

1 Understanding business decision making

Learning outcomes

1.1 Strategy and objectives

Learners need to understand:

- How an organisation sets out and uses:
  - Vision, mission statement, strategy, objectives
- That objectives should be:
  - Specific, measurable, achievable, realistic, time-based
- The importance of non-financial key performance indicators (KPIs)
- Approaches to strategy:
  - Cost leadership, differentiation, focus
- Total Quality Management (TQM)
  - Continuous improvement, right first time, organisation-wide philosophy
- The costs of quality:
  - Prevention, appraisal, internal failure, external failure
- How economic factors affect strategy and performance:
  - Competition, economic growth, government policy, inflation, interest rates, international trade, supply and demand, unemployment

Learners need to be able to:

- Identify whether decisions align with an organisation's:
  - Vision, mission statement, strategy, objectives
- Identify:
  - Effective non-financial KPIs, unintended consequences of non-financial KPIs
- Calculate non-financial KPIs
- Interpret performance using non-financial KPIs
- Identify the ethical implications of decisions.

1.2	**Position analysis**
	Learners need to understand:
	• A SWOT analysis:
	  - Strengths, weaknesses, opportunities, threats
	• The use of a SWOT analysis
	• A PESTLE analysis:
	  - Political, economic, social, technological, legal, environmental
	• The use of a PESTLE analysis.
	Learners need to be able to:
	• Identify:
	  - Strengths, weaknesses, opportunities, threats
	• Identify factors:
	  - Political, economic, social, technological, legal, environmental
	• Recommend action to be taken following:
	  - A SWOT analysis, a PESTLE analysis.

1.3	**Cost-benefit analysis** Learners need to understand: • Cost benefit analysis. Learners need to be able to: • Complete a cost-benefit analysis • Recommend action to be taken following a cost-benefit analysis.

Assessment context

In the Advanced Business Awareness assessment, you should be prepared to analyse business decisions and consider how well they align with an organisation's vision, mission, strategy and objectives. You may need to interpret non-financial KPIs and apply tools such as SWOT, PESTLE and cost benefit analysis to suggest suitable actions in different business situations.

Qualification context

You may have seen aspects of strategy and performance analysis in other AAT units, but the detailed application of strategic tools and environmental analysis is mainly assessed in Advanced Business Awareness. The understanding you build here will strengthen the way you evaluate information and make judgements across the wider Level 4 qualification.

Business context

Businesses operate in environments shaped by competition, economic conditions and global trends. Being able to analyse decisions and assess their strategic impact helps you understand why organisations act the way they do. Using recognised analytical tools supports better decision making, reduces risk and helps organisations respond effectively to opportunities and threats.

Chapter overview

Understanding business decision making

- **Strategy and objectives**
  - Vision, mission, strategy and objectives
  - SMART criteria
  - Critical success factors
- **Key performance indicators (KPIs)**
  - Financial KPIs
  - Non-financial KPIs
  - Balanced scorecard
- **Approaches to strategy**
  - Porter's potential positioning strategies
  - Cost leadership, differentiation and focus
- **Total quality management and costs of quality**
  - Total quality management (TQM)
  - Principles of TQM
  - Costs of quality
- **Economic impacts on strategy and performance**
  - Economic factors
- **Position analysis**
  - PESTLE analysis
  - SWOT analysis
- **Cost benefit analysis**
  - Cost benefit analysis
  - Tangible and intangible costs and benefits

Introduction

Effective decision making sits at the heart of every successful organisation. Whether a business is setting long-term strategic goals, responding to changes in the external environment, or evaluating investment opportunities, the ability to make informed and well-structured decisions is essential to achieving sustainable success.

This chapter introduces the key concepts and tools that underpin business decision making. It begins by exploring how organisations define their **vision, mission, strategy and objectives**, and how these are translated into measurable targets using **key performance indicators (KPIs)**. Understanding how performance is assessed – including the role of **non-financial KPIs** and approaches such as the **balanced scorecard** – is crucial for evaluating whether a business is on track to meet its goals.

The chapter also considers different **approaches to strategy**, including cost leadership, differentiation and focus, alongside the principles of **total quality management (TQM)** and the importance of managing quality-related costs. These concepts highlight how businesses can build competitive advantage while maintaining efficiency and customer satisfaction.

In addition, you will examine how external influences, such as **economic conditions**, can affect organisational performance and strategic choices. Tools such as **SWOT and PESTLE analysis** are introduced to help assess both internal capabilities and the wider business environment, supporting more informed and structured decision making.

Finally, the chapter explores how organisations evaluate specific options using **cost–benefit analysis**, ensuring that decisions are supported by a clear understanding of both financial and non-financial impacts.

Overall, this chapter provides a foundation for understanding how businesses make decisions in practice. By linking strategy, performance measurement, environmental analysis and financial evaluation, it shows how different elements come together to support effective and responsible decision making within a real-world business context.

1 Strategy and objectives

Business organisations make decisions all of the time. Such decisions may be focussed on day-to-day operations (such as when running a factory) or be wider and more long-term in nature (such as deciding whether to enter a new market or not). In this section we shall see that for businesses to be successful, all decisions must be based on what they wish to achieve for the future.

1.1 Vision, mission, strategy and objectives

Different types of organisations have different purposes. These purposes can be broken down into their vision and mission which are supported by strategy and objectives.

KEY TERM

Vision: The desired future state of the organisation. Generally, this will be high level and timeless.

Mission: An expression of overall purpose and scope of the organisation in line with the values and expectations of stakeholders. It answers the question – what sort of business are we or do we want to be?

Strategy: The organisation's plan of how to get from where it is now to where it wants to be in the future.

Objectives: Specific targets that set and control the overall functioning and progress of the organisation in order to meet its strategy.

1.1.1 Vision

An organisation's **vision**, often contained in a **vision statement**, is the organisation's view of where it sees itself going in the long term. Vision sets the organisation's mission, strategy and objectives because these concepts concern the purpose of the organisation and its future.

An example of a **vision statement for a restaurant chain** might be:

'Our vision is to be the preferred destination for guests seeking exceptional dining experiences, recognised for outstanding service, a distinguished wine selection, and restaurants located where our customers live, work, and socialise.'

1.1.2 Mission

An organisation's **mission** is its basic purpose and what it is trying to achieve. It is often set out in a mission statement.

Mission statements often have some of the following characteristics:

- Stating the purpose of the organisation
- Stating the areas in which the organisation intends to operate
- Providing a general statement of the organisation's culture
- Acting as a guide to develop the direction of the organisation's strategy and its goals/objectives

The **content of mission statements** is up to the business itself. Some organisations split their mission statement down into areas such as sustainability, profitability and innovation to give them a structure.

An example of a **mission statement for the restaurant chain** in the example above might be:

'Our mission is to deliver consistently high-quality service in welcoming and conveniently located restaurants, complemented by an extensive and carefully curated wine list. We are committed to creating memorable dining experiences through attentive hospitality, expert wine stewardship, and locations that effortlessly fit into our guests' lifestyles.'

Illustration 1: Mission statements

Think about a global airline. What do you think its mission statement should be?

Solution

An example of a mission statement for a global airline could be:

'To provide high-quality, on-time air travel that allows people to travel in state-of-the-art comfort and style to any location in the world.'

This statement states the purpose of the organisation (to provide air travel), where it operates (around the world), a clue to its culture (state-of-the-art/stylish) and its goals and objectives (high quality and on time).

Assessment focus point

Assessments may give you some information about business operations and ask you to identify which aspect of the mission statement they relate to.

1.1.3 Strategy and objectives

Vision and **mission** set the framework for an organisation's strategy (its plans for achieving its vision and mission). An organisation is likely to have various strategies for different parts of the business, all of which need to be achieved for it to move closer to meeting its vision and mission. For example, if an organisation has a vision of growing to be the market leader, it is likely to have a technology strategy (to ensure that the required investment is made in technology), a marketing strategy (to increase sales) and a human resources strategy (to ensure that it employs enough suitably qualified staff to meet demand).

However, to start implementing the strategy and managing performance, an organisation needs to develop objectives.

Objectives translate a mission into more specific milestones and targets for the business strategy to follow and achieve.

Examples of objectives for our restaurant example might be:

- Maintain a wine list of at least 80 distinct wines per restaurant, including a balanced range of local and international selections, and review and update the list twice per year.
- Open three new restaurant locations in high-footfall, easily accessible areas (eg city centres, transport hubs, or retail developments) within the next 24 months, following formal location feasibility studies.
- Ensure 100% of front-of-house employees complete certified customer service and wine knowledge training within six months of hire, with annual refresher training thereafter.

They have the following functions:

- **Planning**: To define and set out milestones on how the organisation will achieve its mission and vision.
- **Responsibility**: To define the responsibilities of managers and departments.
- **Integration**: To support the other objectives and be consistent (to integrate the efforts of different parts of the organisation).
- **Motivation**: To motivate managers (the first step in motivation is knowing what is to be done). Objectives must be created for all areas of performance.
- **Evaluation**: To provide benchmarks for performance assessment and control.

Some objectives are more important than others. In the hierarchy of objectives, there is a primary corporate objective and other secondary objectives which should combine to ensure the achievement of the overall corporate objective.

Objectives will also differ according to the level within the organisation.

Organisational level	Description
Strategic (corporate) objectives	To set the overall long-term objectives for the business as a whole.
Tactical objectives	To plan and control individual functions within the organisation.
Operational objectives	To act as day-to-day performance targets to ensure that the organisation's operations are carried out efficiently or effectively.

Regardless of where objectives sit in the organisation's hierarchy, they should always be **Specific, Measurable, Achievable, Realistic and Time-based (SMART)**.

SMART Factor	Description
Specific	Objectives should be clear and well defined, focusing on exactly what needs to be accomplished. Being specific removes ambiguity and ensures everyone understands the intended outcome and the steps needed to reach it.
Measurable	A measurable objective includes criteria that allow progress to be tracked and success to be assessed. By defining metrics or indicators, you can determine whether you're on track and know when the goal has been achieved.

SMART Factor	Description
Achievable	Objectives should be realistically attainable with the resources, skills, and time available. An achievable goal stretches capability without becoming unrealistic, helping maintain motivation and commitment.
Realistic	A realistic objective aligns with broader priorities, constraints, and organisational context. It should make sense within the current situation and be feasible given existing limitations, ensuring the goal contributes meaningfully to overall aims.
Time-based	Every objective should include a clear timeframe or deadline. A time-based goal provides urgency, supports planning, and helps maintain focus, ensuring progress is made steadily and completion is clearly defined.

1.1.4 Critical success factors (CSFs)

An organisation may break objectives down into the key areas it must perform well in to achieve its objectives. These are known as **critical success factors (CSFs)**. If an organisation focuses on achieving these CSFs, then it will be well placed to achieve its larger objectives. When developing CSFs, organisations should ensure that some relate to its conditions (eg location) and its capabilities (eg customer service) needed to meet objectives.

Examples of **CSFs for the restaurant chain** that we saw earlier might be:

- Offer a high quality service
- Provide an extensive wine list
- Locate restaurants in convenient locations

2 Key performance indicators (KPIs)

Once an organisation has identified its critical success factors, it should then set performance standards. These are known as **key performance indicators (KPIs)** and are specific, measurable objectives that need to be achieved for the organisation to reach the level of performance that it aspires to.

KPIs can be broadly **categorised** into:

- **Financial KPIs**, such as revenue, profit margins, and return on investment.
- **Non-financial KPIs**, which focus on operational performance, quality, customer satisfaction, innovation, and employee effectiveness.

KPIs are often used for **control purposes,** for example, if KPI targets are not being met, then management action can be taken to resolve the underlying issue and improve the organisation's performance.

While **financial KPIs** remain essential for assessing organisational viability and profitability, they provide only a partial view of performance. The table below sets out some of their **limitations**:

Limitation	Explanation
Historical focus	Financial KPIs are largely lagging indicators, reflecting the outcomes of past decisions rather than providing insight into future performance. For example, revenue figures illustrate what has already happened but do not explain why, for example, customers chose to dine at a restaurant or whether they are likely to return.
Limited insight into operational quality	Financial data does not capture key operational drivers such as service quality, staff competence, customer experience, or brand reputation. A restaurant may achieve short term profitability while simultaneously delivering poor service that undermines long term sustainability.
Risk of short termism	An excessive focus on financial performance can encourage short term cost cutting decisions (eg reducing staffing levels or training budgets) that negatively affect service quality and customer satisfaction.

As a result, relying solely on financial KPIs may obscure emerging problems and fail to support strategic objectives centred on quality and customer experience.

Non-financial KPIs complement financial measures by providing forward-looking and explanatory insights into performance. They are particularly important in service-based industries such as hospitality, where customer experience and service quality are key sources of competitive advantage.

Using our **restaurant example**, non-financial key performance indicators might be:

- Percentage 4 star plus feedback given on online reviews (objective 95%+ 4 star feedback)
- Percentage of customers booking online at least a week in advance (objective 75% booking at least a week in advance)
- Percentage of meals returned to kitchen (objective <5% of meals being returned to kitchen)

The table below sets out some **benefits of non-financial KPIs**.

Benefit	Explanation
Measuring service quality and effectiveness	Non-financial KPIs allow organisations to assess how well strategic objectives are being delivered in practice. For a restaurant chain focused on high quality service, metrics such as customer satisfaction scores or complaint rates provide direct feedback on service effectiveness.
Capturing customer experience and loyalty	Measures such as repeat visit rates, online review ratings, and net promoter scores capture customer perceptions and behaviour, which are strong predictors of future revenue and long term success.

Benefit	Explanation
Supporting continuous improvement and innovation	Non-financial KPIs highlight operational weaknesses and opportunities for improvement. For example, low wine attachment rates may indicate the need for enhanced staff training or improved menu design, rather than pricing changes.
Aligning daily operations with strategy	By focusing on factors employees can influence directly – such as service standards, product knowledge, and responsiveness – non financial KPIs help align staff behaviour with the organisation's critical success factors.

Assessment focus point

Assessment questions may require you to identify and calculate effective non-financial KPIs.

2.1 The balanced scorecard

The balanced scorecard (Kaplan & Norton, 1996) focuses on **four** different perspectives and aims to establish goals for each together with **a combination of financial and non-financial measures** which can be used to evaluate whether these goals have been achieved.

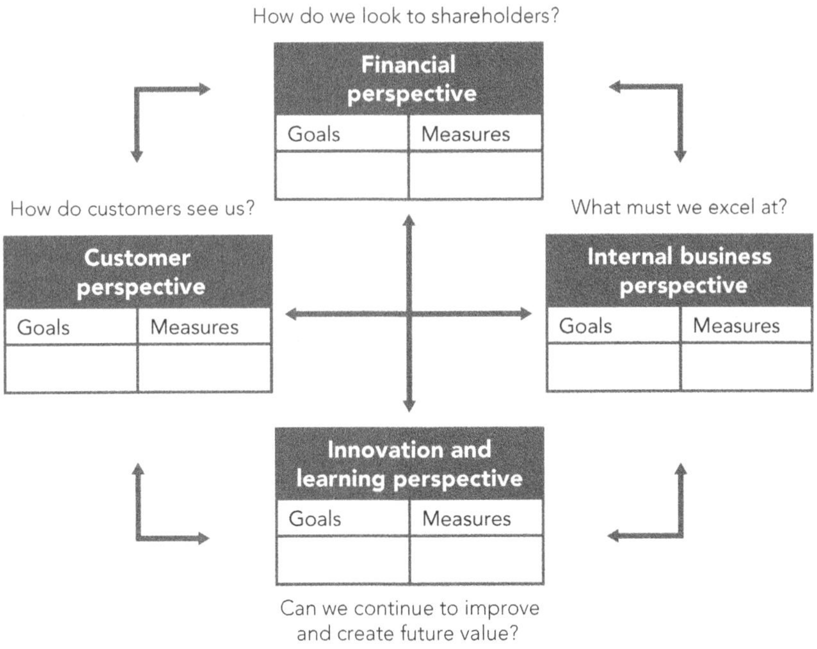

Figure 1.1: The balanced scorecard

Customer measures often focus on quality, delivery time, performance and service.

Internal business measures will focus on processes that are important to meeting **customer expectations** such as quality, time and cost.

Innovation and learning measures are concerned with improving key **internal processes** and creating value for **customers.** Measures often focus on the amount of innovation and the success of innovation, and also achieving long-term targets for improving business processes.

Financial measures – successful strategies should create value for **shareholders.** Measures will normally cover **survival** (cash flow), **success** (sales or profit) and **prosperity** (shareholder value).

2.1.1 Features/benefits of the balanced scorecard

- It links performance measures to key elements of a company's **strategy**.
- It requires a balanced consideration of all **four perspectives**, to prevent improvements being made in one area at the expense of another.
- It considers **financial and non-financial** measures and goals and both **internal** and **external** factors.
- It attempts to establish the needs and concerns of customers in order to identify **new products and markets.**

2.1.2 Problems with using the balanced scorecard

- It can be difficult to select which measures to include, and how many to include. There could be a danger of **information overload**. It is important to only include indicators because they add value, not because they are easy to measure.
- Having a number of different indicators (or too many indicators) can make **interpretation** of overall performance **difficult**. Worse performance in some areas leads to improved performance in other areas (eg higher material costs may cause profits to fall in the short term, but could lead to higher customer satisfaction).
- The needs of internal stakeholders (particularly **staff**) are not explicitly included. Also, the scorecard doesn't take account of **corporate social responsibility** (CSR).

2.1.3 Worked example

ZJET is an airline company that operates both domestically and internationally using a fleet of 20 aircraft. Passengers book flights using the internet or by telephone and pay for their flights at the time of booking using a debit or credit card.

The airline has also entered into profit sharing arrangements with hotels and local car hire companies that allow rooms and cars to be booked by the airline's passengers through the airline's website.

ZJET currently measures its performance using financial ratios. The new managing director has suggested that other measures are equally as important as financial measures and has suggested using the balanced scorecard to identify three non-financial performance measures (**one** from **each** of **three** different perspectives of the balanced scorecard) that ZJET could use as part of its performance measurement process.

A possible solution would be:

Perspective	Measure	Why?
Customer	Number of times customer fails to make a booking due to website crash or busy phone lines	Potential loss of customers
Internal	Number of take-offs on time	Measures efficiency of process
Innovation and learning	Number of new destinations	Attracts more customers to airline

Activity 1: Non-financial and financial objectives

Corporate objectives should relate to the business as a whole and can be both financial and non-financial. Identify the non-financial and financial objectives that may apply for a car manufacturer.

Required

Identify the non-financial and financial objectives that may apply for a car manufacturer.

Objective	
Market share	▼
The quality of the firm's products	▼
New product development	▼
Customer satisfaction	▼
Asset base	▼

Picklist

- Financial objective
- Non-financial objective

Assessment focus point

Be prepared to use KPIs to interpret an organisation's performance or to consider any unintended consequences of using KPIs (for example where basing decisions on a KPI has negative effects elsewhere on the business).

3 Approaches to strategy

When developing its strategy to achieve its long-term vision and mission, an organisation will often consider how to position itself within the market.

KEY TERM

Market positioning: How customers perceive a brand or product relative to other brands or products.

When positioning products and services, most organisations want to achieve a clear, unique and positive position, such as the cheapest supermarket or highest-quality vehicle manufacturer.

Key considerations include the following.

- Many products are, in fact, very similar, and the key issue is to create a distinction in the customer's mind.
- Few products occupy a market space on their own. Inevitably they will be positioned in relation to competing products.
- People remember 'number 1', so the product should be positioned as 'number 1' in relation to a positioning variable.

3.1 Porter's potential positioning strategies

Porter (1980) identified four potential positioning strategies.

	Low cost	High cost
Broad target	Cost leadership	Differentiation
Narrow target	Cost focus	Differentiation focus

Cost leadership means that the business aims to reduce its cost base so that it can produce its goods or services cheaper than its competitors. This will mean that it can charge lower prices than the competition and still be profitable.

Differentiation is where the organisation competes by making its products and services different to what is currently available in the market, for example by ensuring that its products are of a higher quality or have unique and desirable features.

Focus. Porter suggests that cost leadership and differentiation strategies can be applied in a broad or narrow range of the market. The narrower the range of the market, the greater degree of focus. Therefore, organisations that operate in small niches of a market have a focus strategy.

Activity 2: Positioning

For an industry of your choice, think about who the main organisations are and what their positioning strategies might be.

4 Total quality management and costs of quality

An **organisation's approach to quality** is an important aspect to its strategy. We have just seen that quality can be part of a position strategy of differentiation and differentiation focus. It is perhaps not so important to organisations who follow cost leadership, as customers who accept lower prices often accept this may mean that the goods or services they buy are of lower quality than higher priced alternatives.

Traditional views on quality management suggest that for an organisation to **consistently** deliver products and services of the level of quality expected by its customers (or other key stakeholders), it must:

(a) Establish acceptable **quality standards** (eg defect rates)

(b) **Design procedures** to delivery this level of quality

(c) **Monitor** actual quality

(d) **Take control action** if quality falls below standard

This means that traditionally, organisations have accepted that a certain level of defective products is inevitable and therefore the best approach is to monitor quality levels and take action to correct issues as they arise (for example scrapping defective products that are identified in quality control procedures). An alternative approach to this traditional view is **Total Quality Management** (TQM).

4.1 Total Quality Management (TQM)

Increasing demands from customers for high quality and increasingly competitive markets has led to a **change** in manufacturing (and service provision) away from simply minimising production costs and inspecting quality.

The **increased emphasis on high quality, highly customised output,** producing exactly what is wanted by the customer when they want it (ie with minimal inventory) is sometimes referred to as 'world class manufacturing'. A key part of this approach is 'total quality management' (TQM).

Quality management becomes **TQM when:**

(a) **Quality standards are set to an extremely high level** (eg zero defects); and

(b) Emphasis is placed on **resolution of problems that cause poor quality** rather than just detecting and correcting problems with quality as they emerge.

KEY TERM

> **TQM:** 'An integrated and comprehensive system of planning and controlling all business functions so that products or services are produced which meet or exceed customer expectations. TQM is a philosophy of business behaviour, embracing principles such as employee involvement, continuous improvement at all levels and customer focus [...]' (CIMA Official Terminology).

4.1.1 Principles of TQM

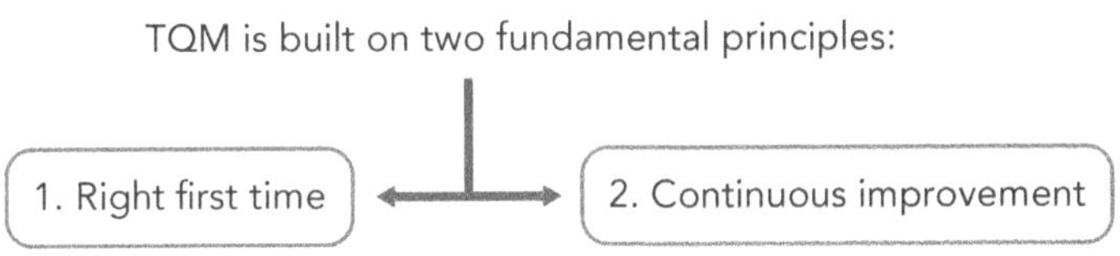

Principles of TQM

Right first time

The **cost of preventing mistakes is usually less than the cost of correcting them** after they occur, so the aim should be **to get things right first time.** Every mistake or delay directly costs an organisation money through **wasted time and effort**, and **lost potential for future sales.**

TQM moves away from relying on inspecting to achieve a predefined level of quality to **preventing the cause** of **any defect** in the first place. To achieve this, TQM requires an awareness by **all personnel** of their role in meeting the customer's quality requirements.

Measures to support 'right first time'	
Control of suppliers	Suppliers are given a rating for their quality levels, with preference given to well-rated suppliers. This method is referred to as 'vendor rating'. It is the **supplier's responsibility to carry out the necessary quality checks**, or face cancellation of the contract.

Measures to support 'right first time'	
Internal customers	TQM builds a recognition that the **customer-supplier relationship** extends to **internal customers**: passing substandard material to another division is not acceptable. Some organisations **formalise this** by requiring each internal supplier to make a **service level agreement** (SLA) with its internal customer. An SLA is a statement of the standard of service that will be provided to the internal customer and will cover the range of services supplied, response times and dependability.
Employee empowerment	**Empowerment** has two key aspects: (a) Allowing workers to have the **freedom to decide how to do** the necessary work, using the skills they possess and acquiring new skills as necessary to be an effective team member (b) Making workers **responsible** for achieving production targets and for quality control
Product and process design	This may involve: (a) Reducing the **number of parts** – the fewer the number of parts to be designed, purchased and assembled the lower the chance of errors (b) Using parts or materials that are **already used** by other products; the more common parts used, the less chance there is of a product failing (c) **Production engineering:** the **process of designing the methods for making a product** (or service) **to the design specification** – it sets out to make production methods as efficient as possible This may involve **computer-aided design (CAD).**

Continuous improvement

It is **always possible to improve** processes, and TQM emphasises the need for employees work together (often in cross-departmental 'quality circles') to make incremental improvements to reduce waste and thereby reduce costs.

TQM aims to foster a consistent, systematic approach to continuous improvement that involves every aspect of the organisation.

4.1.2 Organisation-wide philosophy

We have seen that for TQM to be a success, all employees and departments need to be involved. The whole organisation must buy into an **organisation-wide philosophy** that quality matters and to follow the TQM principles. Adopting TQM involves the organisation moving away from the traditional approach to quality. This means, for example, it will no longer rely on quality control checks to identify quality issues. Therefore, if not all employees or departments adopt the TQM philosophy, quality issues will occur and are less likely to be identified and corrected.

4.2 Costs of quality

Quality management programmes, such as TQM, often involve considerable time and expense.

A cost of quality report helps to assess the success of quality programmes.

The cost of quality can be analysed into the following categories:

Prevention cost	Appraisal cost	Internal failure cost	External failure cost
Costs incurred prior to or during production in order to prevent substandard or defective output from being produced.	Costs incurred in order to check that outputs produced meet required quality standards.	Costs arising from inadequate quality which are identified **before** the transfer of ownership from supplier to purchaser.	Costs arising from inadequate quality discovered **after** the transfer of ownership from supplier to purchaser.
Examples: • Preventative repairs and maintenance • Training in quality control • Time spent discussing quality issues (quality circles)	Examples: • Acceptance testing • Inspection of goods inwards	Examples: • Repair costs • Losses from failure of purchased items	Examples: • Administration of customer complaints section • Costs of repairing products returned from customers • Lost sales

These costs could be applied to our **restaurant example** as follows:

Prevention costs – Staff training, recruitment and selection of highly knowledgeable staff, pre-emptive maintenance of kitchen equipment.

Appraisal costs – Mystery diners to assess service quality, customer satisfaction surveys, supervisor checks of food and drink to customer orders before service.

Internal failure costs – Detecting incorrect wine being selected before serving, staff checking bills before presenting them to the customer, ensuring the correct number of tables and place settings for each reservation before the customer arrives.

External failure costs – Free meals or drinks offered to appease unhappy customers, reductions to the bill due to poor service (such as long wating times for food), loss of repeat customers.

The cost of the quality management programme is the total of **prevention and appraisal costs**. These are sometimes called conformance costs.

The **internal and external costs of failure** are sometimes called non-conformance costs; these costs should fall if a quality management programme is succeeding.

It is likely that there will be a **trade-off between expenditure in these two categories** – ie the greater the spend on conformance costs, the lower the resulting non-conformance costs should be.

The total cost of quality measures whether the investment in conformance costs is paying off in the form of lower non-conformance costs.

Illustration 2: Cost of quality

Y Co's quality costs for the most recent period are as follows:

Cost type	£
Performing supplier quality ratings	250,000
Sample check of quality of finished products	45,000
Equipment to measure chemical composition of products	75,000
Warranty claims	840,000
Cost of re-inspecting goods that have been re-worked	25,000

Required

What is Y Co's current level of appraisal costs?

	✓
$45,000	
$120,000	
$370,000	
$145,000	

Solution

The correct answer is:

	✓
$45,000	
$120,000	✓
$370,000	
$145,000	

The answer is calculated as $45,000 + $75,000 = $120,000.

	$	
Performing supplier quality ratings	250,000	Prevention cost – allows best quality suppliers to be used and quality issues to be prevented
Sample check of quality of finished products	45,000	Appraisal cost
Equipment to measure chemical composition of products	75,000	Appraisal cost – form of inspection
Warranty claims	840,000	External failure cost
Cost of re-inspecting goods that have been re-worked	25,000	Internal failure – only necessary due to non-conformance

5 Economic impacts on strategy and performance

Businesses do not exist in isolation, they are part of, and are therefore affected by, the wider business environment. This environment is not static, but changes everyday. These changes impact an organisation's progress in meeting its strategies, and therefore business decisions often involve reacting to changes in the business environment to keep the organisation on track. One of the key aspects of the business environment is the economy.

5.1 Management of the economy

Macro-economics describes the wider economy that all businesses and industries operate in within a particular country. It includes factors such as taxation, interest rates, employment levels, inflation and economic growth.

Economic factors affecting strategy and performance	Explanation
Competition	The level of competition between organisations in the economy for sales. Competition levels rise where there are many firms in comparison to the number of available customers. Prices for goods or services in highly competitive markets are often driven down by the competition which means that only organisations with a low cost-base are likely to survive in the long-term.
Economic growth	Economic growth occurs where more goods and services are produced by the economy, and society becomes better off. Several factors contribute to the creation of economic growth, for example low interest and taxation rates, as well as a low unemployment rate. These factors create conditions where those living within the economy have more spare income to spend. This increases demand for goods and services as people look for opportunities to spend their money.
Government policy	Government spending policy directly impacts the economy because the levels of money spent (or not spent) by the government are so great. The formal planning of fiscal policy (ie tax and spend policies) is set out annually (eg in the UK in the 'Budget') which has three components: • Expenditure planning • Revenue raising • Borrowing If a government decides to use fiscal policy to influence demand in the economy, it can choose either expenditure changes or tax changes as its policy instrument. Demand can be increased by government: • Reducing taxation, but does not change its spending, then demand is stimulated • Spending more, but not altering taxation Demand can be reduced by government: • Increasing taxation or reducing spending As well fiscal and monetary policy, governments have policies on a range of other areas. For example, it may have a policy on grants (money that the government provides to encourage investment in certain areas).

Economic factors affecting strategy and performance	Explanation
	For example, grants are currently available in the UK for customers to purchase electric vehicles or heat pumps for their homes. In each case, the government pays a fixed part of the cost of an electric vehicle or heat pump, making the cost of investment cheaper to the customer and encouraging them to make a purchase.
Inflation	Inflation is the name given to an increase in price levels generally. A consequence of inflation is the decline in the purchasing power of money (for example £10 will buy you more goods today than it will in 10 years' time). Inflation is caused by several factors, for example where demand for goods is greater than supply (demand pull inflation) or where the costs of production (such as employee pay or energy costs) increase and are reflected in the prices organisations charge (cost-push inflation).
Interest rates	Interest rates are the 'price' of money. A nation's central bank (in the UK it is the Bank of England) usually sets a central interest rate, (for example 5%). This interest rate drives the interest rates charged by banks to their customers for borrowing and what they pay customers for their savings. Because banks want to make money themselves, they often charge borrowers a higher rate of interest than the central bank rate and pay savers a lower rate of interest than the central bank. Interest rates form part of the government's monetary policy and are a key factor in controlling demand and inflation within the economy. For example, where interest rates are high, people and businesses pay more interest on their borrowing and so have less disposable income to spend on goods and services, reducing demand and therefore inflation.
International trade	International trade is the trade between the economy and nations outside of the economy. This trade may be buying in raw materials from overseas or selling products or services to overseas markets. International trade operates in a similar way to trade within an economy, but other factors will also impact it. For example, rules and regulations may affect what can and cannot be traded, or in what quantities. Another key aspect of international trade is exchange rates. Exchange rates are the value of one nation's currency in comparison to other nations.

Economic factors affecting strategy and performance	Explanation
	'Strong' currencies benefit from being able to buy in goods and services from overseas at a lower cost. This benefits importers, but will negatively affect exporters who may find selling goods and services overseas difficult because their goods and services will be relatively more expensive for someone in the overseas market to buy compared to locally produced alternatives. The reverse is true for 'weak' currencies. Governments may develop an international trade policy (for example to increase the country's exports and reduce its imports. The purpose of doing this would be to generate growth in the country by increasing demand for products made within the country.
Supply and demand	Demand is the quantity of a good that potential purchasers would buy, or attempt to buy, if the price of the good were at a certain level. Supply is the quantity of a good that existing suppliers or would-be suppliers would want to produce for the market at a given price. Demand and supply determines the price for goods and services. An 'equilibrium price' occurs where the price customers are willing to pay is the same as the price that suppliers are willing to sell at. As levels of demand and supply change, so the market price of a good or service will change too.
Unemployment	Unemployment occurs where people within an economy are available to work but there is no job for them to do. It is often expressed as a percentage: (Number of unemployed/Total workforce) x 100 Not all people who live in an economy are included within the total workforce. For example, students, retired people, those with long-term health conditions that prevent them working and those who look after family members at home are often excluded. Flows into unemployment are: • Members of the working labour force becoming unemployed (for example, redundancies, lay-offs, voluntary quitting job) • People who were previously not part of the labour force joining the unemployed (such as recently qualified students without a job, and carers rejoining the workforce but having no job yet).

Economic factors affecting strategy and performance	Explanation
	Flows out of unemployment are: • Unemployed people finding jobs • Laid-off workers being re-employed • Unemployed people stopping the search for work Unemployment results in the following problems. • Loss of output. If labour is unemployed, the economy is not producing as much output as it could. Thus, total national income is less than it could be. • Loss of human capital. If there is unemployment, the unemployed labour will gradually lose its skills, because skills can only be maintained by working. • Increasing inequalities in the distribution of income. Unemployed people earn less than employed people, and so when unemployment is increasing, the poor get poorer. • Social costs. Unemployment brings social problems of personal suffering and distress. For example, an increased risk of social unrest as well as issues such as theft and vandalism. • Increased burden of welfare payments. This can have a major impact on government fiscal policy.

6 Position analysis

For an organisation to make good decisions it is important that it understands the position that it finds itself in within the business environment, this includes the economic situation, but other important aspects as well.

6.1 Analysing the environment

6.1.1 Elements of the environment

The business environment can be described as **everything which is beyond the organisational boundary.**

Management cannot control the environment; however it influences all aspects of organisational activity and so the organisation's relationship with the environment must be viewed strategically. It comprises a number of different elements:

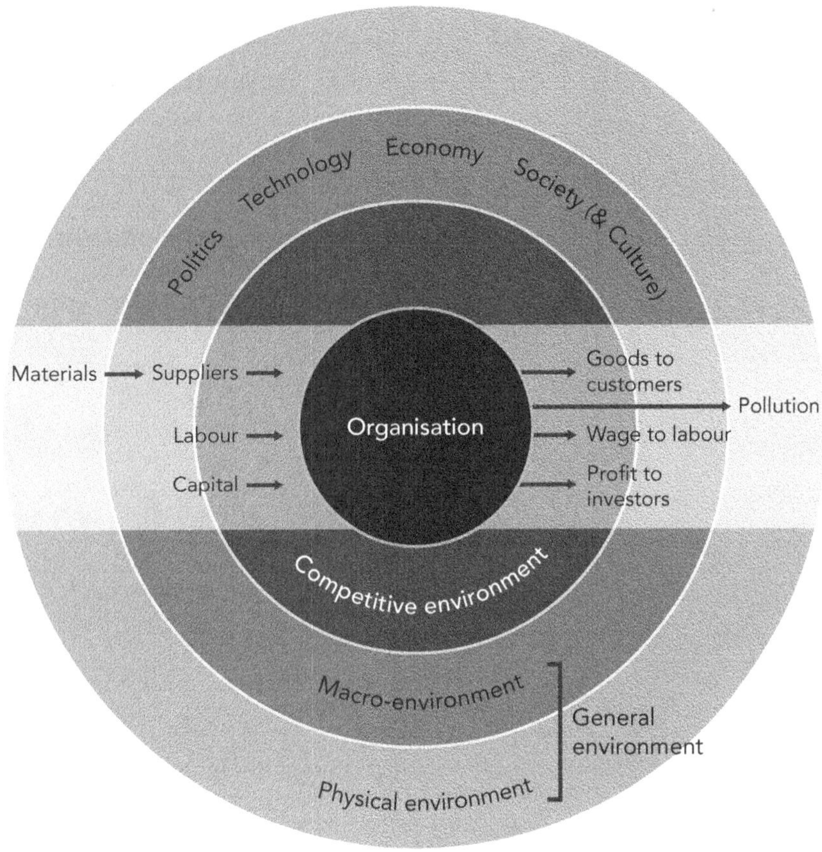

The general environment covers all the **political/legal, economic, social/cultural, natural environment** and **technological** influences in the countries in which an organisation operates.

6.2 PESTLE analysis

PESTLE analysis is used as a framework for identifying the factors that influence the business environment:

PESTLE area	Description
P Political	Government policy influences the economic environment, the framework of laws, industry structure and certain operational issues. Political instability is a cause of risk, because it means that the assumptions under which the business has made its longer-term plans may change, and so impact on the business' ability to achieve its objectives. Different approaches to the political environment apply in different countries. International trade is subject to a further layer of international law and regulation.
E Economic	The economic factors that we saw previously (such as inflation, interest rates, taxation, unemployment, growth and demand and supply) which impact the business.

PESTLE area		Description
S	Social/Cultural/Fashion	Changes in social attitudes impact the demand for goods and services, and so opportunities open up or close down as fashions and trends change.
T	Technology	Information systems and information technology has a significant role in the development of the modern business environment and on business strategy. For example, it can create new products and services to sell or improve the efficiency and effectiveness of business processes.
L	Legal	National and international laws and regulations affect the operating activities of most organisations, for example: • Anti-discrimination legislation • Health and safety legislation • Product safety and standardisation • Employment rights • Training and education policies
E	Environmental	There is increasing concern about businesses' relationship with the natural environment. Businesses may suffer significant costs and a loss of reputation if problems arise. Much business activity takes place at some cost to the environment. Examples of impacts on the environment include: • Depletion of natural resources • Noise and aesthetic impacts • Residual air and water emissions • Long-term waste disposal • Uncompensated health effects • Change in the local quality of life Failing to take sufficient account of environmental impact can have a significant impact on the business as well as the outside world.

6.2.1 Using a PESTLE analysis

The PESTLE analysis can be used in one of two ways.

(a) An organisation can use PESTLE to **identify external environmental factors** that may influence strategic decision-making. By analysing political, economic, social, technological, legal, and environmental factors, the firm can anticipate changes in the macro-environment and assess how these may affect future performance. For example, changes in minimum wage legislation or licensing laws may impact cost structures or operating hours in the hospitality sector.

(b) The business can use PESTLE to **identify opportunities and threats arising from the external environment** and develop strategies to respond to them. In other words, by understanding how external trends such as changing consumer preferences, technological advancements in online reservations, or increased demand for sustainable practices are evolving, the organisation can adapt its strategy to exploit opportunities and minimise potential risks.

6.3 SWOT analysis

The section above discussed the **external environment** and the factors that might affect organisations. As part of the strategic planning process, organisations may analyse the **internal** and **external environments,** and then summarise these using SWOT analysis.

SWOT analysis is a method of environmental analysis which looks at an organisation's **internal strengths** and **weaknesses** as well as **external opportunities** and **threats**:

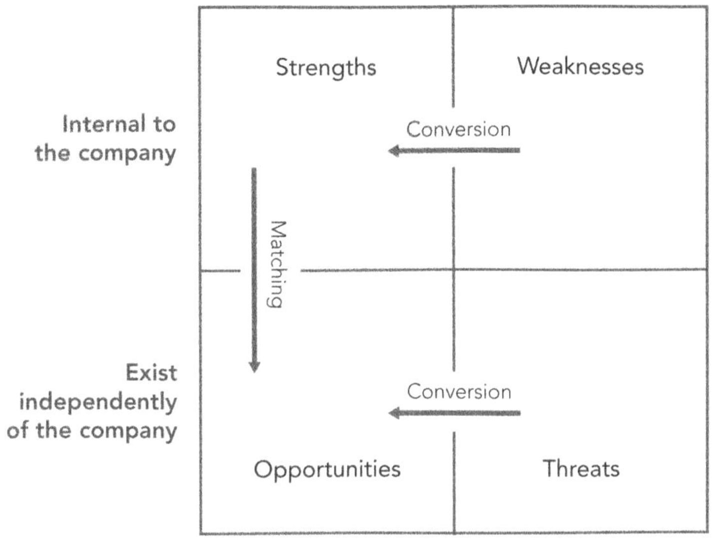

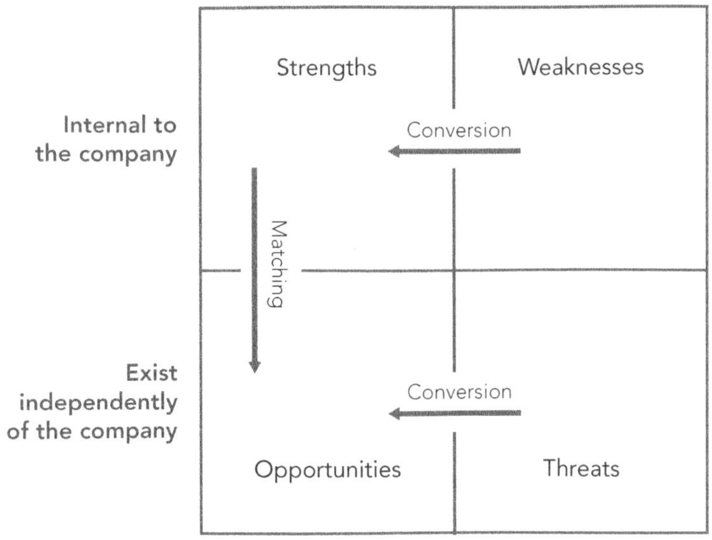

6.3.1 Strengths and weaknesses

An internal appraisal will identify:

(a) The areas of the organisation that have **strengths** that should be exploited by suitable strategies

(b) The areas of the organisation that have **weaknesses.** Businesses can either avoid strategies that might be affected by their weaknesses, or find ways to overcome them – for example developing new capabilities. This is what is meant by converting weaknesses into strengths.

The strengths and weaknesses analysis is intended to shape the organisation's approach to the external world. For instance, the identification of shortcomings in products could lead to a programme of product development.

6.3.2 Opportunities and threats

The external appraisal identifies **opportunities** that can be exploited by the organisation's strengths and anticipates environmental **threats** against which the company must protect itself.

Opportunities

(a) What opportunities exist in the business environment?

(b) What is their inherent profit-making potential?

(c) Can the organisation exploit the worthwhile opportunities?

(d) What is the comparative capability profile of competitors?

(e) What is the company's comparative performance potential in this field of opportunity?

Threats

(a) What threats might arise to the company or its business environment?

(b) How will competitors be affected?

(c) How will the company be affected

It may be possible to turn a threat into an opportunity by developing new strategies to overcome the threat that may lead to greater opportunities.

6.3.3 Using a SWOT analysis

The SWOT analysis can be used in one of two ways.

(a) The organisation can develop **resource-based strategies** which enable the organisation to extend the use of its strengths. For example, a supermarket chain extends its range of own branded goods from food to other areas.

(b) The business can develop **positioning-based strategies**. In other words, identifying what opportunities are available and what the firm has to do to exploit them.

> **Assessment focus point**
>
> Assessments may require you to identify PESTLE or SWOT factors from a scenario or recommend suitable actions following such analysis.

7 Cost benefit analysis

KEY TERM

> **Cost benefit analysis:** Analysis of the costs and benefits to an organisation of a potential business decision.

Business decisions often impact the **organisation's costs**. For example, investment in a new information system will mean significant costs to the business for purchasing, installing and operating the system. However, by making the investment, the business expects **certain benefits** to be gained (such as cost savings due to making processes more efficient, or the creation of better information in future which will lead to better business decisions.

The purpose of a cost benefit analysis is to analyse decisions in terms of the costs and benefits to the organisation. For a decision to go ahead, the benefits of the decision should outweigh the costs.

Both costs and benefits can be tangible and intangible.

KEY TERM

> **Tangible costs:** Identified, quantifiable costs relating to a decision (such as the cost of new office equipment).
>
> **Intangible costs:** Costs that cannot be quantified in financial terms (such as the cost of lost customers if a new system is not introduced). These costs are often difficult to identify and quantify.

Tangible benefits: Benefits to the business of making the decision (such as improved efficiency) that are easy to identify. However, they may be hard to quantify precisely, and estimates or projections will be open to debate.

Intangible benefits: Other benefits of the decision, which are both difficult to identify and quantify. For example, an improved business reputation or better customer experience).

A simple **cost-benefit analysis** may look something like this:

	£'000	£'000
Initial costs		
Cost of machinery	500	
Staff training	75	
Site preparation	10	
		585
Annual running costs		
Safety checks (req'd every 2100 hours of production)	150	
Replacement drill heads	14	
		164
Total costs over lifetime (5 years)		749
Savings		
Staff hours savings	25	
Costs of running the old machinery (5 × 155)	775	
		800
Total net benefit over 5 years		51

In order to produce an accurate and meaningful cost-benefit analysis, it is necessary to ensure all costs and benefits are included.

Activity 3: Cost benefit analysis

Your organisation is considering installing self-service kiosks in its reception area to allow visitors to sign in, print badges, and automatically notify staff when their guests arrive. This would reduce the amount of time reception staff spend on routine check-in tasks and aims to create a smoother, more modern visitor experience.

The proposal involves purchasing two kiosks costing £14,000 in total, along with an annual software subscription of £1,200. The IT department estimates that setup and configuration will require 30 hours of work, and their average hourly cost is £28 per hour. Reception staff will also need to attend a half-day training session, and their average hourly pay is £18 per hour. The training session lasts 4 hours and will involve three staff members.

Management predicts that once implemented, the kiosks will reduce reception workload by around 70 hours per month, allowing staff to redirect their time towards other tasks. They also expect that faster check-ins will improve first impressions for visitors and reduce queuing at busy times. However, they are aware that some visitors may initially struggle with the new system and that a few reception staff members may prefer the current process.

Required

(a) Calculate the total tangible costs of the project for the first year.

£ [ ]

(b) Which of the following is an intangible benefit of introducing the new self-service kiosks?

	✓
Reduced reception workload by 70 hours per month	
Improved first impressions for visitors due to smoother check in	
Annual software subscription cost of £1,200	
Increased staff availability for other administrative tasks	

Assessment focus point

Be prepared to perform a cost-benefit analysis (with calculations) or to recommend an appropriate course of action following a cost-benefit analysis.

Chapter summary

- Business organisations make **decisions** all of the time. Such decisions may be focussed on **day-to-day operations** (such as when running a factory) or be wider and more **long-term** in nature (such as deciding whether to enter a new market or not).
- An **organisation's vision**, often contained in a vision statement, is the organisation's view of where it sees itself going in the long term.
- An **organisation's mission** is its basic purpose and what it is trying to achieve. It is often set out in a mission statement.
- **Objectives** translate a mission into more specific milestones and targets for the business strategy to follow and achieve.
- Regardless of where objectives sit in the organisation's hierarchy, they should always be **Specific**, **Measurable**, **Achievable**, **Realistic** and **Time-based** (SMART).
- **Key performance indicators (KPIs)** are specific, measurable objectives that need to be achieved for the organisation to reach the level of performance that it aspires to.
- The **balanced scorecard** (Kaplan & Norton, 1996) focuses on four different perspectives and aims to establish goals for each together with a combination of financial and non-financial measures which can be used to evaluate whether these goals have been achieved.
- **Porter** (1980) identified four potential positioning strategies, **cost leadership**, **differentiation** and **focus**.
- **Total quality management (TQM)** is an approach to quality that moves away from relying on inspecting to achieve a predefined level of quality to preventing the cause of any defect in the first place. It is an organisation-wide philosophy based on the principles of right first time and continuous improvement.
- Quality costs can be categorised as **prevention costs**, **appraisal costs** and **internal** and **external failure costs**.
- **Macro-economics** describes the wider economy that all businesses and industries operate in within a particular country. It includes factors such as taxation, interest rates, employment levels, inflation and economic growth.
- **PESTLE analysis** is used as a framework for identifying the factors that influence the business environment.
- **SWOT analysis** is a method of environmental analysis which looks at an organisation's internal strengths and weaknesses as well as external opportunities and threats.
- **Cost benefit analysis** analyses of the costs and benefits to an organisation of a potential business decision.

Activity answers

Activity 1: Non-financial and financial objectives

Objective	
Market share	Financial objective
The quality of the firm's products	Non-financial objective
New product development	Non-financial objective
Customer satisfaction	Non-financial objective
Asset base	Financial objective

Activity 2: Positioning

The answer to this activity will be based on the industry you have chosen.

As an example, the UK supermarket industry has several major organisations that compete. Lidl and Aldi are examples of cost leaders who keep their costs as low as possible so that they can compete aggressively on price with their rivals. Waitrose and Marks and Spencer are examples of organisations that follow a differentiation strategy. They differentiate their products through marketing their products as being of higher quality, more sustainable and higher welfare for meat and fish products.

Activity 3: Cost benefit analysis

(a) £ 16,256

The total tangible costs come to £16,256, made up of the kiosk purchase (£14,000), the annual software subscription (£1,200), IT setup and configuration (30 hours at £28/hour = £840), and staff training (three staff for four hours at £18/hour = £216). These figures represent all the direct, measurable financial costs associated with installing and implementing the self-service kiosk system.

(b) The correct answer is:

	✓
Reduced reception workload by 70 hours per month	
Improved first impressions for visitors due to smoother check in	✓
Annual software subscription cost of £1,200	
Increased staff availability for other administrative tasks	

This option is correct because improved first impressions and smoother check ins relate to perceptions and visitor experience, which cannot be directly measured, making them an intangible benefit. Reduced reception workload is incorrect because reduced reception workload is a measurable, numerical saving, so it is a tangible benefit. Annual software subscription cost is incorrect because the software subscription is a cost, not a benefit. Increased staff availability for other administrative tasks is also incorrect because increased staff availability can be measured in hours gained, making it a tangible benefit rather than an intangible one.

Test your learning

1 **Complete the statement below:**

[▼] is/are the organisation's view of where it sees itself going in the long term

Picklist

- Mission
- Objectives
- Strategy
- Vision

2 **Which perspective of the balanced scorecard is concerned with improving key internal processes and creating value for customers?**

	✓
Customer	
Internal business	
Innovation and learning	
Financial	

3 **Which of the following is NOT a macro-economic issue?**

	✓
Employment levels	
The volume of goods businesses are willing to supply	
Interest rates charged by banks	
Level of aggregate demand	

4 **Complete the statement below:**

Governments may provide financial incentives for investment in certain areas. Such incentives are known as [▼] .

Picklist

- Benefits
- Bonuses
- Grants
- Interest
- Tax rebates

5 **Which aspects of SWOT analysis focus on factors internal to the organisation?**

	✓
Strengths	
Weaknesses	
Opportunities	
Threats	

2 Understanding organisational effectiveness

Learning outcomes

2.1 Personal effectiveness

Learners need to understand:

- Effective time management using the Eisenhower matrix
- The steps that can be taken to ensure communication is accurate and appropriate
- The consequences of inaccurate or inappropriate communication
- The importance of:
  - Collaboration, escalation, delegation

Learners need to be able to:

- Identify action to be taken using the Eisenhower matrix
- Recommend when to:
  - Collaborate, escalate, delegate
- Recommend:
  - Types of business communication
  - Improvements to existing business communication
- Use reflective practice to enhance effectiveness

2.2 Equity, diversity and inclusion (EDI)

Learners need to understand:

- The meaning of:
  - Equity, diversity, inclusion, unconscious bias
- The benefits of an inclusive and diverse workforce
- The challenges to implementing EDI policies
- Actions that can be taken to promote EDI by:
  - Organisations, individuals

Learners need to be able to:

- Recommend actions to take to promote EDI

Assessment context

In the assessment, you may be expected to review scenarios involving communication, teamwork and time management. You should be prepared to identify when it is appropriate to collaborate, escalate or delegate, and to recognise issues related to equity, diversity and inclusion.

Qualification context

Although communication and teamwork appear throughout the qualification, this chapter is where these skills are explored in depth. The knowledge you gain here will support you when engaging with tasks in other Level 4 units, particularly those that require clarity in communication or effective working practices, such as Audit and Internal Controls.

Business context

Organisations rely on individuals who can manage priorities, communicate clearly and work effectively with others. Strong personal effectiveness helps prevent errors and supports productive working relationships. As businesses respond to technological developments, sustainability objectives and changes in markets, your ability to adapt and support change can contribute to a positive and resilient workplace.

Chapter overview

Understanding organisational effectiveness

- **Personal effectiveness**
  - Time management
  - Planning your time
  - Prioritising plans with the Eisenhower matrix
  - Communication as a finance professional
  - Communicating effectively, clearly and appropriately
  - Impact and consequences of ineffective or inappropriate communication
  - Types of business communication
  - Collaboration
  - Escalation
  - Delegation
  - Reflective practice
- **Equity, diversity and inclusion (EDI)**
  - Equity (equality)
  - Diversity
  - Inclusion
  - Equity, diversity and inclusion (EDI) policies
  - Unconscious bias

Introduction

Organisational effectiveness is about how well a business achieves its objectives by making the best use of its people, processes and resources. While strategy sets the direction of an organisation, it is the effectiveness of individuals and teams that determines whether those objectives are successfully delivered in practice.

This chapter focuses on two key areas that underpin effectiveness in a modern business environment: **personal effectiveness** and **equity, diversity and inclusion (EDI)**.

It begins by exploring how individuals can improve their own performance through effective **time management, planning and prioritisation**, including the use of tools such as the **Eisenhower matrix**. The chapter also highlights the importance of **clear and appropriate communication**, particularly within a professional context, and considers the potential consequences of ineffective communication. Alongside this, you will examine when to **collaborate, escalate or delegate tasks**, and how **reflective practice** can be used to continuously improve performance.

The chapter then broadens its focus to consider how organisations create an inclusive and supportive working environment through **equity, diversity and inclusion (EDI)**. You will develop an understanding of key concepts such as **equity, diversity, inclusion** and **unconscious bias**, and explore the benefits that a diverse workforce can bring to organisational performance. It also considers the challenges organisations may face in implementing EDI initiatives, and the actions that both organisations and individuals can take to promote an inclusive culture.

By linking individual performance with organisational culture, this chapter demonstrates how effectiveness is achieved not only through efficient working practices, but also through fostering a positive and inclusive environment. These elements are essential for improving productivity, supporting ethical behaviour, and enabling organisations to operate successfully in a diverse and dynamic business context.

1 Personal effectiveness

Organisations are only effective if individuals who work for them are effective in their work. In this section we shall look at how individuals can be effective in terms of their time management and communication, as well as consider other important aspects such as collaboration, escalation and delegation.

1.1 Time management

Everyone has a fixed and limited amount of **time** available to them and there are various demands placed on your time from your work life and non-work life. Therefore, time is an important **resource** time that needs to be managed if it is to be used efficiently (without waste) and effectively (productively).

1.2 Planning your time

The diagram below sets out the key principles of time management. They can be used to plan your workload whilst at work, but they can also be applied to aspects of your non-work life as well.

The **key principles of time management** (Adair, 2009) can be summarised as follows.

- **Goals** – identify what you want to achieve (to know when you have achieved them).
- **Action plans** – decide how you intend to achieve your goals (factors such as timescale, deadlines, tasks involved and resources required).
- **Priorities** – decide which tasks are the most important (for example which would be the most valuable use of your time) and tackle them in that order.
- **Focus** – when working, concentrate on one thing at a time. Ensure that everything you need is available and prevent interruptions if you can.
- **Urgency** – work on any task you are doing as if it was needed soon (do not put tasks off because you think they are too complex or large).
- **Organisation** – create positive work habits which minimise wasted time and effort. Do similar tasks together and manage your to-do list to avoid letting tasks 'pile up'.

Tasks can be classified in several ways, for example as routine, unexpected, urgent and important.

KEY TERM

Routine tasks: Tasks which you perform almost daily and are most likely set out in your job description (for example, processing expenses, performing bank reconciliations or creating financial reports).

Unexpected tasks: Tasks that do not occur on a daily basis. For example, they may be one-off special jobs, such as covering for an employee who is on leave or assisting a colleague to meet an important deadline. Although unexpected, these tasks are still part of general working life, and you will need to fit them into your work schedule. To do this you will need to adjust your plans and priorities to take account of changing demands.

Urgent tasks: Tasks that must be completed for a deadline in the near future. For example, the Marketing Director may request a breakdown of sales by product for a meeting first thing tomorrow morning.

Important tasks: Tasks that have major value or potential consequences for the organisation: for example, preparing an investment appraisal for a major project, or information needed for a board meeting.

A task will be classed as important if:

- Other people or tasks rely on its timely completion (a task which is relatively unimportant to you may be an important part of someone else's work);
- The consequences of non-completion are high (in terms of costs, damage, delay); and/or
- It has been requested by an individual or body which has high power (eg a senior manager or government agency).

It is natural to think that an urgent task is important – or that an important task is urgent – but this is not necessarily the case. You may have time to devote to the important task – or you may have to 'drop' an urgent task because it is not as important as another requirement. This is a question of priority.

1.2.1 Prioritising plans with the Eisenhower matrix

All tasks (even routine ones) should be **planned**, even if it is just to decide the order in which you will carry them out. Such planning becomes even more valuable when unexpected tasks are given to you, since you now need to juggle more tasks than before and some might be more urgent or important than others. The process of determining the order in which tasks should be carried out is known as **prioritising**.

Common-sense tells you that urgent tasks should have a higher priority than non-urgent tasks (because they are required first), and that important tasks are higher priority than unimportant tasks (for example because information required for a directors meeting has more value to your organisation than you working through routine email queries.

The **Eisenhower Decision Matrix** (Covey, S. 1990) is a useful tool that helps prioritise tasks. To use this tool, you should allocate your tasks into four categories and each category is given a different priority:

Category	Explanation
Urgent and important	Tasks that must be done in the very near future and which are important to you and to other people in the organisation. (For example, you are asked to produce a report for a manager for a high-level strategy meeting tomorrow morning.)
Not urgent but important	Tasks which are important but not immediately due. (For example, today is Monday and the project manager has asked for some product costings for Friday.) Beware, however; if you leave non-urgent tasks too long, they become urgent!
Urgent but not important	Tasks which are urgent – but will not be a major problem if not completed in time. (For example, there is no milk in the kitchen, and the shops are about to close. The worst that can happen is some grumbling, until you can find time to shop the following morning.)
Not urgent and not important	Tasks that can be slotted into the gaps between higher-priority tasks. (For example, periodically you may pack up out of date files to be stored in the archives.)

This model is a good starting point to put your tasks into priority order, but you will still need to also prioritise tasks which are all in the **same category** (for example if you have four urgent and important tasks to do).

If tasks are of **equal urgency and importance**, or there are no particular issues of priority, the following are some other possible criteria for determining the order in which tasks should be completed.

- **Arrival time**: performing tasks in the order in which they are requested.
- **Most nearly finished**: starting with the task nearest completion. (It is satisfying ticking off finished tasks – and frustrating to interrupt a nearly complete task to start something else.)
- **Shortest task first**: enabling you to get lots of tasks out of the way quickly.
- **Longest/most difficult task first**: enabling you to get some momentum on tasks you might otherwise procrastinate over!
- **Difficulty of handover**: if you are about to go on holiday, say, you should tackle the things that it will be most difficult for someone else to take over while you are away.

Remember, that just because you have planned your tasks for a day or a week it does not mean that your plans cannot change. Other unexpected tasks can (and will) come along. This will require you to be flexible and to change your priorities to meet the current situation.

Assessment focus point

Assessments may require you to apply the Eisenhower matrix to help identify appropriate actions to take in a set of given circumstances.

Activity 1: Routine or unexpected tasks

Place each of the tasks in the picklist in the relevant box below.

Routine tasks	Unexpected tasks
▼	▼
▼	▼
▼	▼

Picklist

- Helping your manager prepare a report as the deadline has been made earlier
- Preparing a weekly petty cash report
- Preparing an aged receivables report
- Reconciling the accounts payables ledger when the accounts payable clerk is off sick
- Responding to customer emails regarding their sales account
- Welcoming a visitor for your manager when your manager has been called into an urgent meeting

1.3 Communication

As well as good time management skills, to be an effective finance professional you also need to be effective in the **preparation**, **giving** and **receiving** of **information**.

1.3.1 Communication as a finance professional

Communication is the **transmission** or **exchange of information**: putting across a message. However, there are many different purposes for doing this:

Reason	Explanation
To inform	To give people information that they require (such as providing management accounts for directors).
To persuade	To get others to agree to, or do, something (for example demonstrating that a project is financially viable by providing evidence in the form of an investment appraisal report).
To request	To ask for something (such as emailing a colleague to provide you with some sales data for a report you are writing).
To confirm	To check that data is correct and that different parties have the same understanding of it (for example providing a summary of a recent discussion to set out action points that were agreed).
To build effective working relationships	Communication is the foundation of relationships between colleagues.

1.3.2 Effective communication

Communication is a two-way process that can be thought of as a 'cycle'. The **communicator** sends a message (or signal) to the **recipient,** who sends back confirmation that the message has been received and understood.

In a business setting, some methods of communication are more appropriate and effective than others. Letters, memos, emails, reports, notes, phone calls and meetings are all valid means of communication, but that does not mean that they are always appropriate or effective in the circumstances. You will need to consider factors such as whether speed is important; whether there is the need for written confirmation; which format will best support you in getting your message across to the recipient; and which is the most efficient method in terms of time and cost for example.

1.3.3 Communicating effectively, clearly and appropriately

To **work effectively** you need to demonstrate that you can communicate effectively, clearly and appropriately in a range of work-related tasks. So, what makes communication effective, clear and appropriate?

Attribute	Explanation
Using appropriate formats and language	Selecting the right format (letter, email, memorandum etc) for the job and ensuring that the content is sensitive to the needs and feelings of those who will receive the communication and to those who the communication concerns.
Observing format conventions and house style	Using formats correctly: observing conventions of structure, format and style, within organisational guidelines and 'house style' (the company's preferred manner of presentation). Standard templates and guidelines are useful to improve the consistency of an organisation's communication.
Professionally presented	Ensuring that documents are neat, legible, concise, helpfully structured and smartly presented: showing competence and awareness of business needs
Technically correct	Ensuring that content is accurate, appropriately detailed (for different levels of requirement) and checked for factual/data and typographical errors
Clearly understandable	Tailored to the writer's purpose in communicating (so that a clear message is sent) and to the information needs, language and capabilities of its audience (so that the message can be received)
Projecting the appropriate corporate image	Reflecting a general image of professionalism and competence – including appropriate formality – and the specific desired image or 'character' of the organisation
Achieving its purpose	Obtain feedback to check that the communication has been effective. Has it 'done its job'? Has it got the response it aimed for? If not: adjust and try again!

1.3.4 Impact and consequences of ineffective or inappropriate communication

If the information you produce is ineffective or inappropriate, then it will have **several consequences.**

- The message you are communicating may not be received by the other person or they may misunderstand what the message is.
- The other person may have to unnecessarily spend more time trying to understand what you are saying which means they will have less time to spend on their work.
- Poorly presented information may reflect badly on you as a professional and on your organisation's corporate image.
- The information may not achieve its purpose.
- Efficient working and constructive working relationships may be damaged.

Assessment focus point

Assessments may require you to consider business communications that have taken place, or are planned to take place, to identify the consequences of that communication. For example, the impact on employees if they are to be told by an instant message that the business is making redundancies.

1.4 Types of business communication

The following table summarises some common types of business communication. It is likely that you will have encountered them, and others (such as meetings, telephone calls and noticeboards) in your earlier studies or in your work environment.

Type of communication	Description
Business letter	A letter is a very flexible and versatile medium of written, person to person communication. It can be used for many business purposes: requesting, supplying and confirming information and instructions; offering and accepting goods and services; conveying and acknowledging satisfaction and dissatisfaction (eg complaint and adjustment letters); and explaining what else is in an information package via a covering letter. In many cases, the business letter has been replaced by email, either as the email itself or as a document attached to it.
Email	Emails are a method for sending electronic messages from one computer to another, either internally within the workplace or to an external party. Email is easy to use, extremely fast and relatively cheap. It is also particularly flexible, because photos, diagrams, computer files or spreadsheets can be sent (with the email as a kind of 'covering letter') as attachments.

Type of communication	Description
Business reports	A report is a general term, which covers a wide range of formats. If you inform someone verbally or in writing of facts, events, actions you have taken, or suggestions you wish to make – you are reporting. In this sense, you can make a report in a meeting or phone call, letter, memo or email. If you are asked for an informal report, however, this will usually mean a relatively short written document, in which information is presented in a direct and structured way. A formal report however can be a massive, complex and highly structured affair, presenting and analysing high-level concepts and information.
Spreadsheets	A spreadsheet is essentially an electronic piece of paper divided into rows and columns with a built-in pencil, eraser and calculator. It provides an easy way of performing numerical calculations and presenting information. The intersection of each column and row of a spreadsheet is referred to as a cell. A cell can contain text, numbers or formulae. Use of a formula means that the cell which contains the formula will display the results of a calculation based on data in other cells. If the numbers in those other cells change, the result displayed in the formula cell will also change accordingly. With this facility, a spreadsheet is used to create financial models.
Social media	The use of social media apps such as X, Facebook, YouTube and Instagram to communicate quick, often highly visual messages to those who follow the organisation's account.
Meetings	Business meetings can be hosted online (such as through Zoom or Teams) as well as being held face-to-face. Online meetings have the advantage that they can be setup at short notice and do not require attendees to travel, however, face-to-face meetings have the advantage that they allow better communication and for business relationships to be enhanced.

Type of communication	Description
Messaging and online	Messaging apps such as Teams and Slack allow colleagues to instantly communicate with each other and allow decisions to be made quickly and recorded in the App. Businesses may also offer online portals on their websites or Apps that allow customers or other stakeholders to send messages to the business.
Intranets	An intranet is used to disseminate and exchange information 'in-house' within an organisation. The idea behind an intranet is that companies set up their own mini version of the Internet. Each employee has a browser, used to access a server computer that holds corporate information on a wide variety of topics, and in some cases also offers access to the Internet.

Activity 2: Communication mediums

Suggest the most effective medium for communication in the following situations using the picklist.

Situation	Medium
The CEO wishes to send a message to all employees.	▼
A member of staff based at the same office as their manager is due their annual performance appraisal.	▼
New IT consumables are required from the office goods supplier.	▼
A team needs to decide how to collectively approach a project.	▼

Picklist

- Face to face conversation
- Meeting
- Notice board/intranet
- Online

1.5 Collaboration, escalation, delegation and reflective practice

In this final section on personal effectiveness we shall now consider the importance of collaboration, escalation, delegation and reflective practice.

KEY TERM

Collaboration: The process of working jointly with colleagues, departments, or stakeholders to achieve a shared objective. It involves combining skills, knowledge, and resources to produce outcomes that are better than what individuals could achieve alone.

Escalation: The process of raising an issue, risk, or concern to a more senior person or appropriate authority when it cannot be resolved at the current level or within your responsibility.

Delegation: The process where one person (often a superior) gives another (often a subordinate) part of their own authority to make decisions or to perform a task.

1.6 Collaboration

In modern organisations, finance professionals rarely work in isolation. Financial decisions affect operations, HR, procurement, marketing, and senior leadership, so effective collaboration ensures that financial information is understood, used, and trusted by others. **Collaboration** also supports stronger problem solving, as financial staff often need input from non-financial teams to produce accurate budgets, forecasts, and analysis.

Good collaboration **builds positive working relationships,** reduces conflict, and supports a culture of accountability and transparency. For personal effectiveness, it demonstrates professionalism, adaptability, and an understanding that finance plays a strategic role across the whole organisation.

1.7 How collaboration helps a finance professional be effective

Collaboration:

- **Improves accuracy** of financial work by ensuring information is shared openly and checked with other departments.
- **Strengthens decision-making**, as input from different teams provides context behind financial data.
- **Builds trust and credibility** with colleagues who depend on finance for guidance.
- **Supports smooth workflows** because issues are addressed jointly rather than in isolation.
- **Reduces misunderstandings** through clear, collaborative communication.
- **Encourages innovation**, as combined perspectives can lead to better solutions to financial or operational problems.
- **Increases efficiency**, preventing duplicated work and ensuring teams pull in the same direction.

1.8 Escalation

In finance roles, escalation **protects the organisation** by ensuring that **problems** such as cost overruns, non-compliance risks, errors, or missing information are **addressed early** by those who can take corrective action. It requires judgement: knowing when an issue is beyond your expertise, when a risk could affect deadlines or accuracy, or when a situation needs managerial approval.

Effective escalation involves clear communication, presenting relevant information, and explaining why the issue needs higher-level intervention. As a personal effectiveness skill, it shows responsibility, awareness of organisational structure, and the ability to prioritise the organisation's needs over personal hesitation.

1.9 How escalation helps a finance professional be effective

Escalation:

- **Prevents small issues from becoming major** financial or operational risks.
- **Ensures compliance**, especially in areas like procurement rules, financial controls, and regulatory requirements.
- **Protects deadlines**, for example when delays or missing data could disrupt reporting.
- **Demonstrates professional judgement** – knowing when to seek guidance rather than acting beyond authority.
- **Supports accurate financial outputs,** because errors or uncertainties are addressed promptly.
- **Strengthens risk management**, allowing senior staff to intervene early.
- **Shows accountability and transparency**, building trust across the organisation.

Activity 3: Collaboration and escalation

Which of the following is the most appropriate action when a team member encounters a problem that is blocking progress on a shared project?

	✓
Continue working alone and wait to see if the problem resolves itself.	
Ask the team for input and escalate to the project lead if the issue cannot be resolved together.	
Immediately escalate the issue to senior management without discussing it with the team.	
Ignore the issue and move on to another task to avoid delays.	

1.10 Delegation

In the workplace, some individuals are permitted to **delegate** their work. Delegation is where an individual **passes over work** that they are responsible for to another individual to complete. Delegation is based on the following four attributes:

(a) Authority – the **right** to do something

(b) Responsibility – the **obligation** to get something done

(c) Accountability – the **readiness to accept responsibility**, judgement by others

(d) Power – the **ability** to do something

Delegation enables management to allocate **responsibility** and **authority** to others, whilst retaining overall accountability.

It is the role of the manager to **take responsibility** and **organise people** to get things done. This involves the use of **authority** and **power** and implies a hierarchy in which power is delegated downwards while accountability is rendered upwards.

When tasks are delegated, any authority and power is usually delegated as well. However, the person delegating the task still has overall **responsibility** and **accountability** for the work which is done on their behalf.

1.10.1 Methods of delegating

Delegation can be done via **several different methods**:

Method	Comment
Abdication	Involves just leaving issues, with no formal delegation. This is not usually a very effective method.
Custom and practice	Involves building delegation into the fabric of the organisation, eg the most junior member of staff collects the mail.
Explanation	The delegator briefs the subordinate on the work that needs to be done.
Consultation	Involves discussion before delegating. This can be an effective method in identifying the best way to get the work done.

1.10.2 Benefits of delegation

Delegation has **several key benefits**:

- There are **physical and mental limitations** to the workload of any individual or group in authority.

- Individuals are freed up to concentrate on **higher-level tasks** (such as planning).
- The **increasing size and complexity** of some organisations calls for specialisation, both managerial and technical.
- Delegated authority contributes to the **job satisfaction and development** of lower level employees. Taking on progressive levels of responsibility supports training, appraisal and management succession planning.
- **Delegation shortens the chain of decision making** and brings decisions closer to the situations that require them. This is particularly important in fast-changing business environments that require responsiveness to customer demands.

1.10.3 Reluctance to delegate

Some individuals may be **reluctant to delegate tasks**. For example, if they:

- Believe that their **colleagues lack the skills** or experience to perform the task.
- **Do not understand** how or what to delegate.
- **Fear a loss of control** over their responsibilities.
- Believe that **performing routine tasks helps them stay in touch** with what is happening in their department.
- **Fear that their colleague will do a better job** than they can.
- Feel that they could **perform the task quicker themselves.**

1.10.4 Effective delegation

Koontz and O'Donnell (1976) explained the requirements of effective delegation:

- **Define the scope of authority** that is delegated to the colleague
- Be satisfied that the **colleague is competent** to be given the delegated authority.
- **Be disciplined** to let the colleague perform the task without constantly checking on them.

It is important that the individual does not delegate so much that their colleague cannot cope with the work, or that it appears that they are just passing work over for someone else to do without good reason. They should make sure that the necessary authority is also delegated and that all individuals that need to know that the work has been delegated are aware of it. Where the individual thinks appropriate, coaching and mentoring should be provided and the delegator should monitor and control the work from a distance.

Assessment focus point

Assessment questions may provide you with a brief scenario and ask you whether actions are required to collaborate, escalate or delegate.

1.11 Reflective practice

KEY TERM

Reflective practice: The habit of taking time to look back on your actions, decisions, and outcomes to understand what went well, what could have been improved, and what you can do differently next time. It encourages individuals to pause, think, and learn from real experiences rather than simply moving from task to task on autopilot.

For finance professionals, reflective practice is especially valuable because the role involves complex decision making, interpreting data, managing risk, and communicating insights to others. By regularly reflecting on completed analyses, stakeholder conversations, report quality, or project outcomes, finance professionals can identify patterns in their work – strengths to build on and areas where new skills or approaches may be needed. This not only boosts personal confidence and accuracy but also leads to clearer judgement, better collaboration with colleagues, and more reliable financial insights for the organisation.

Ultimately, **reflective practice** creates a **cycle of continuous improvement**. It helps finance professionals stay adaptive, sharpen their analytical thinking, and deliver higher quality outputs that support better organisational decisions.

2 Equity, diversity and inclusion (EDI)

The previous section considered how individuals who work for an organisation can be effective in their work on a personal level. In this section we shall see how organisations can support their employees to be the best that they can be in a professional sense, but also in a personal sense as well. Many organisations have **equity, diversity and inclusion (EDI) policies** to achieve this.

The purpose of these policies is to recognise that **all employees** (and **potential employees**) have something positive to offer the organisation, even if it is not obvious at first. These policies help ensure that everyone has opportunities to further their career, develop and contribute to the business regardless of their personal circumstances.

2.1 Equity

KEY TERM

> **Equity:** An approach to the management of people at work based on equal access and fair treatment, irrespective of their background (for example, their gender, race, ethnicity, age, disability, sexual orientation and religious belief).

Employers that promote equity **will seek to redress inequalities** (eg of **access to jobs, training, promotion, pay** or **benefits**) that are based around differences, where they have no relevance to work performance. Equity rules apply to both those **working for an organisation** and those **making job applications** to it.

2.1.1 Discrimination

Equity practices originated in **equality laws** that were developed to address **discrimination in the workplace**. There are **four main types of discrimination**:

Type of discrimination	Description
Direct discrimination	Occurs when one interested **group is treated less favourably than another.** It is unlikely that a prospective employer will practise direct discrimination without being aware of it.
Indirect discrimination	Occurs when **a policy or practice is fair in form, but discriminatory in operation**. For example, requiring all applicants to be clean shaven would put members of some religious groups at a disadvantage.
Victimisation	Occurs when **a person is penalised for giving information or taking action** in pursuit of a claim of discrimination.
Harassment	Is the use of **threatening**, **intimidatory**, **offensive** or **abusive language** or **behaviour**.

2.1.2 Benefits of equity to an organisation

Equity brings a number of **benefits to an organisation**. For example:

- **Improved performance and productivity**: Employees who feel supported and treated fairly are more motivated, more engaged, and able to work to their full potential.
- **Stronger talent attraction and retention**: Equitable organisations are more appealing to skilled applicants and are better at retaining high-quality staff who feel valued and fairly treated.
- **Better decision-making**: When barriers are removed, a wider range of people contribute ideas and perspectives, leading to more balanced, well-informed decisions.
- **Higher levels of trust and morale:** Equity creates a sense of fairness and transparency, which increases trust in leadership and strengthens team cohesion.

- **Reduced conflict and grievances:** Fair processes limit the likelihood of disputes, misunderstandings, and formal complaints, saving time and resources.
- **Enhanced reputation**: Organisations with strong equity practices are seen as responsible, ethical, and forward-thinking, improving their brand and stakeholder relationships.
- **Stronger compliance and risk management:** Equity supports consistent, defensible decision-making, helping organisations meet legal and regulatory requirements around fairness and discrimination.

2.2 Diversity

KEY TERM

> **Diversity:** A concept which recognises and respects the fact that every individual is different and has their own unique characteristics.

2.2.1 Managing diversity

A **'managing diversity' orientation** implies the need to be **proactive in managing the needs of a diverse workforce** in such areas such as:

- **Tolerance** of individual differences
- **Communicating effectively** with (and **motivating**) **ethnically diverse workforces**
- Managing workers with **increasingly diverse family structures** and **responsibilities**
- Managing the **adjustments to be made by an increasingly aging workforce**
- Managing increasingly **diverse career aspirations/patterns** and **flexible working**
- Dealing with **differences in literacy**, **numeracy** and **qualifications** in an international workforce
- Managing **co-operative working in ethnically diverse** teams
- **Create diversity training programmes** to help employees better understand each other, benefiting communication and collaboration
- Understanding the **needs of different cultures**
- Promoting acceptance of **social differences**

2.2.2 Benefits of diversity to an organisation

A **diverse organisation** brings together people with different backgrounds, perspectives, skills and experiences – and this variety creates a **stronger,** more **adaptable workforce**. Diversity helps teams think more creatively, spot risks and opportunities earlier, and make better decisions because problems are viewed from multiple angles rather than a single way of thinking. It also improves an organisation's ability to understand and serve a wide range of customers, making products and services more relevant and appealing.

Diverse workplaces also tend to be more **attractive to talented candidates**, helping the organisation recruit and retain skilled people. When employees feel included and respected (perhaps through **employee resource groups**), **engagement** and **morale increase**, which leads to **higher productivity** and **lower staff turnover**. Overall, diversity strengthens innovation, decision making, reputation and staff wellbeing – all key ingredients for long term organisational success.

2.3 Inclusion

KEY TERM

> **Inclusion:** The practice of creating a workplace where everyone feels respected, valued, and able to contribute fully, regardless of their background or personal characteristics. It's not just about having a diverse workforce (the mix of people) or ensuring fairness (equity); inclusion is about making sure every individual feels they belong and can participate meaningfully.

While **diversity** is about who is in the room, and **equity** is about giving people the support they need to have fair opportunities, **inclusion** is about making sure people feel comfortable speaking up, sharing ideas, and being themselves at work. This makes inclusion an active, ongoing process – not something that happens automatically just because a workplace hires a diverse workforce.

For example, **rotating employees through different roles** enables all employees to feel welcome and valued in different areas of the business.

An **inclusive workplace** encourages **open communication,** values **different viewpoints**, and **removes barriers** – formal or informal – that could prevent people from contributing. It has numerous benefits to individuals and the organisation as a whole.

Benefits of inclusion	Explanation
Encourages open communication	Inclusive environments make it easier to ask questions, challenge assumptions, and share concerns – essential for accuracy in financial work.
Improves collaboration with other departments	When everyone feels respected and listened to, teams are more willing to share data, provide context, and work together effectively.
Strengthens decision making	Inclusive practices ensure a wide range of perspectives are considered, helping finance professionals understand the full picture behind financial results.
Builds trust and professional relationships	When colleagues feel valued, they are more likely to trust and cooperate with finance staff, making processes smoother and more reliable.
Supports continuous learning	An inclusive culture makes it easier to admit mistakes, ask for help, and develop skills – key components of personal growth.
Better employee engagement, stronger retention, improved problem solving, and more innovative thinking	These outcomes benefit the organisation directly by creating a more stable workforce, clearer information flows, and better informed business decisions.

2.3.1 Employee resource groups

Employee Resource Groups (ERGs) are voluntary, employee-led groups that bring people together around shared characteristics, interests, or experiences – such as culture, disability, gender, LGBTQ+ identity, parenting, or early-career development. In relation to EDI, ERGs play an important role in creating a more inclusive workplace by giving employees a space to connect, share insights, and raise issues that may otherwise go unheard. They also help organisations understand the needs of different groups, improve policies, and support a culture where everyone feels valued and represented.

2.4 Equity, diversity and inclusion (EDI) policies

As organisations recognise the benefits that **equity, diversity and inclusion** can bring, many will establish **equity, diversity and inclusion (EDI) policies** to formally set out its intentions, plans and rules that are designed to help it achieve its EDI goals.

Sound **business arguments** can be made for having an **EDI policy**. Reasons include:

- **Common decency** and **fairness**, in line with business ethics.
- Good **HR practice**, to **attract** and **retain** the **best people for the job**, regardless of background.
- **Compliance** with **relevant legislation** and **Codes of Practice**, which are applied by employment tribunals.

- **Inclusive hiring practices** will benefit the business by allowing access to a wider pool of skills, experiences and perspectives.
- Improving the business's **image as a good employer** and earning the **loyalty of customers** who benefit from (or support) **equity practices**.

KEY TERM

Equity, diversity and inclusion (EDI) policies: A policy sets out an organisation's commitment to treating everyone fairly, valuing differences, and ensuring that all employees feel respected and able to contribute. It provides guidance on preventing discrimination, promoting equal opportunities, and creating a workplace culture where diverse perspectives are encouraged and supported.

Organisations often face several **challenges** when putting an EDI policy into practice, such as:

Challenge	Explanation
Changing established behaviours and culture	Long standing habits and informal norms can be hard to shift, and staff may need time, support, and training to adapt.
Lack of awareness or understanding	Employees and managers may not fully grasp what EDI means in day to day actions, leading to inconsistent application.
Resistance to change	Some individuals may feel uncomfortable or threatened by new expectations, especially if they believe it adds extra workload or scrutiny.
Ensuring leadership accountability	EDI initiatives only succeed when leaders model inclusive behaviour – and securing this commitment can be challenging.
Gathering and using data appropriately	Organisations need accurate information to track progress, but collecting sensitive data must be handled legally and ethically.
Embedding EDI into everyday processes	Recruitment, promotion, team meetings, and performance management all need to reflect EDI principles, which requires coordinated effort.
Unconscious bias	Covered later in this chapter.

Both organisations and individuals can (and have a responsibility) contribute to the promotion of the EDI. The table below summarises some of the actions that can be taken.

Actions by the organisation	Actions by the individual
Create and communicate a clear EDI policy so everyone understands expectations and values.	Actively challenge unfair behaviour or assumptions when they see them.
Provide regular training to build awareness, challenge bias, and improve inclusive behaviours.	Listen to and value different perspectives, making space for quieter voices in discussions.
Review recruitment and promotion processes to ensure fairness, accessibility, and diverse representation.	Reflect on personal biases and seek opportunities to improve understanding and behaviour.

Actions by the organisation	Actions by the individual
Encourage open communication by creating safe channels for staff to raise concerns or suggestions.	Use inclusive language to help create a respectful and welcoming atmosphere.
Celebrate diversity through events, awareness days or internal campaigns that reflect the workforce.	Learn about different cultures and backgrounds to build stronger, more empathetic working relationships.
Collect and analyse workforce data to identify gaps and track progress in a responsible, ethical way.	Be open to feedback about communication and behaviour, using it to grow and improve.
Hold leaders accountable for modelling inclusive behaviours and championing EDI initiatives.	Support team initiatives that encourage fairness, accessibility and inclusion.

2.5 Unconscious bias

KEY TERM

Unconscious bias: The automatic, unintentional attitudes, beliefs, or assumptions that influence decisions and behaviour without us being aware of them. These biases develop over time through our experiences, culture, and environment, and can affect how we perceive people or situations even when we aim to be fair and objective.

In a business environment, unconscious bias can **subtly influence** recruitment, promotion, teamwork, and everyday interactions. Because these biases operate below conscious awareness, individuals may believe they are being impartial even while unintentionally favouring or disadvantaging certain people or groups. This can lead to unfair decisions, reduced innovation, poor communication, and a workplace culture that feels exclusionary or inconsistent.

2.5.1 Impacts of unconscious bias on EDI goals

Unconscious bias directly affects how well an organisation can achieve its EDI goals.

- **Equity** involves fair access, opportunities, and treatment – but unconscious bias can create hidden barriers that prevent fair outcomes even when policies appear neutral.
- **Diversity** focuses on having a workforce with varied backgrounds, perspectives, and experiences – but unconscious bias can limit who is hired, promoted, or listened to.
- **Inclusion** requires that everyone feels valued and able to contribute – yet bias can lead to certain voices being ignored or certain groups feeling less welcome.

Addressing unconscious bias strengthens EDI by ensuring decisions are based on evidence and capability rather than assumptions. Strategies such as structured decision making, diverse interview panels, reflective practice, and active questioning of first impressions help individuals make more objective choices.

Activity 4: Equity, diversity and inclusion

Which of the following best demonstrates an organisation actively promoting Equity, Diversity and Inclusion (EDI)?

	✓
Treating everyone exactly the same regardless of their needs or circumstances.	
Recruiting people only through word of mouth to ensure cultural fit.	
Expecting staff to resolve EDI concerns informally without involving managers.	
Providing regular EDI training and ensuring policies are applied consistently across all teams.	

Assessment focus point

Assessments may focus on practical aspects of EDI. For example, identifying and recommending suitable actions to promote EDI in an organisation, as well as the benefits and challenges such actions may bring.

Chapter summary

- Everyone has a fixed and limited amount of **time** available to them and there are various demands placed on your time from your work life and non-work life. Therefore, time is an important resource time that needs to be managed if it is to be used efficiently (without waste) and effectively (productively).
- Tasks can be classified in several ways, for example as routine, unexpected, urgent and important.
- The **Eisenhower Decision Matrix**(Covey, S. 1990) is a useful tool that helps prioritise tasks. To use this tool, you should allocate your tasks into four categories and each category is given a different priority:
- As well as good time management skills, to be an effective finance professional you also need to be effective in the **preparation**, **giving** and **receiving** of **information**.
- **Collaboration** is the process of working jointly with colleagues, departments, or stakeholders to achieve a shared objective. It involves combining skills, knowledge, and resources to produce outcomes that are better than what individuals could achieve alone.
- **Escalation** is the process of raising an issue, risk, or concern to a more senior person or appropriate authority when it cannot be resolved at the current level or within your responsibility.
- **Delegation** is the process where one person (often a superior) gives another (often a subordinate) part of their own authority to make decisions or to perform a task.
- **Reflective practice** is the habit of taking time to look back on your actions, decisions, and outcomes to understand what went well, what could have been improved, and what you can do differently next time.
- **Equity** is an approach to the management of people at work based on equal access and fair treatment, irrespective of their background (for example, their gender, race, ethnicity, age, disability, sexual orientation and religious belief).
- **Diversity** is a concept which recognises and respects the fact that every individual is different and has their own unique characteristics.
- **Inclusion** is the practice of creating a workplace where everyone feels respected, valued, and able to contribute fully, regardless of their background or personal characteristics.
- An **equity, diversity and inclusion (EDI) policy** sets out an organisation's commitment to treating everyone fairly, valuing differences, and ensuring that all employees feel respected and able to contribute. It provides guidance on preventing discrimination, promoting equal opportunities, and creating a workplace culture where diverse perspectives are encouraged and supported.
- **Unconscious bias** is the automatic, unintentional attitudes, beliefs, or assumptions that influence decisions and behaviour without us being aware of them.
- **Equity, diversity and inclusion** bring many benefits to an organisation and its employees and there are actions that both organisations and individuals can take to promote them. There are challenges to implementing an EDI policy but they can be overcome.

Activity answers

Activity 1: Routine or unexpected tasks

Routine tasks	Unexpected tasks
Preparing a weekly petty cash report	Helping your manager prepare a report as the deadline has been made earlier
Preparing an aged receivables report	Welcoming a visitor for your manager when your manager has been called into an urgent meeting
Responding to customer emails regarding their sales account	Reconciling the accounts payables ledger when the accounts payable clerk is off sick

Activity 2: Communication mediums

Situation	Medium
The CEO wishes to send a message to all employees.	Notice board/intranet
A member of staff based at the same office as their manager is due their annual performance appraisal.	Face to face conversation
New IT consumables are required from the office goods supplier.	Online
A team needs to decide how to collectively approach a project.	Meeting

Activity 3: Collaboration and escalation

The correct answer is:

	✓
Continue working alone and wait to see if the problem resolves itself.	
Ask the team for input and escalate to the project lead if the issue cannot be resolved together.	✓
Immediately escalate the issue to senior management without discussing it with the team.	
Ignore the issue and move on to another task to avoid delays.	

Asking the team for input and then escalating to the project lead when needed encourages collaboration, shared problem solving, and timely escalation. This approach supports personal effectiveness by ensuring the individual does not stay stuck, and it supports organisational effectiveness by keeping the project moving and involving the right people at the right time.

Working alone and hoping the issue 'sorts itself out' reduces collaboration and risks further delays. This harms both personal productivity and the organisation's workflow. Escalating straight to senior management skips the team and project lead, which can cause unnecessary disruption and undermine normal escalation routes. Effective escalation means starting at the right level. Ignoring the issue can create bigger problems later. It prevents collaboration, delays resolution, and can negatively affect project outcomes and team effectiveness.

Activity 4: Equity, diversity and inclusion

The correct answer is:

	✓
Treating everyone exactly the same regardless of their needs or circumstances.	
Recruiting people only through word of mouth to ensure cultural fit.	
Expecting staff to resolve EDI concerns informally without involving managers.	
Providing regular EDI training and ensuring policies are applied consistently across all teams.	✓

Providing regular EDI training and applying policies consistently shows that the organisation is actively building awareness, reducing bias, and embedding fair practices. This strengthens trust, creates a more inclusive culture, and ensures staff feel supported – all key elements of effective EDI implementation.

Treating everyone exactly the same ignores individual needs and differences. Inclusion requires flexibility – for example, making reasonable adjustments or offering support tailored to specific circumstances.

Recruiting only through word of mouth limits diversity and reduces access for candidates from different backgrounds. It can reinforce existing biases and restrict opportunities for under represented groups.

Expecting staff to deal with EDI concerns informally can prevent serious issues from being addressed. Proper reporting and managerial involvement are essential to ensure concerns are handled fairly and safely.

Test your learning

1 **For each of the following tasks, select their priority category from the picklist.**

Task	Category
Preparing a bank reconciliation by the end of next week	▼
Deleting old or actioned emails	▼
Preparing a document needed for a directors meeting in the morning	▼
Buying tea and coffee for the staff break room when they have run out	▼

Picklist

- Not urgent but important
- Not urgent or important
- Urgent and important
- Urgent but not important

2 **Which of the following best demonstrates effective communication for a finance professional?**

	✓
Sharing financial reports only when asked to avoid overwhelming colleagues	
Presenting complex financial information in clear, accessible language tailored to the audience	
Using as much technical terminology as possible to sound professional	
Sending emails instead of speaking to colleagues to save time	

3 **Which of the following shows the most effective use of delegation in a finance role?**

	✓
Completing all analysis personally to ensure accuracy, even when team members have capacity.	
Passing on tasks you find uninteresting without offering support or context.	
Assigning part of a financial review to a junior colleague, providing clear guidance and checking progress at agreed points.	
Delegating critical decisions to colleagues without confirming whether they have the necessary skills.	

4 **Which of the following best describes diversity in the workplace?**

	✓
Having a workforce made up of individuals with different backgrounds, perspectives, and experiences	
Employing people only from groups that are under represented	
Ensuring every employee receives identical support regardless of their needs	
Allowing managers to choose team members based solely on personal preference	

5 **Which of the following best describes the purpose of an organisation's EDI (Equity, Diversity and Inclusion) policy?**

	✓
To ensure all employees receive the same training, regardless of their need	
To create fair access, remove barriers, and support a workplace where different people can contribute fully	
To prioritise diversity targets over employee performance	
To ensure only HR is responsible for managing workplace behaviour	

3 Understanding ethics and law in an accounting environment

Learning outcomes

3.1 Ethics and professional scepticism

Learners need to understand:

- The difference between:
  - Law and ethics
- The meaning of:
  - Personal ethics, business ethics, professional ethics
- The interrelationship between:
  - Law, ethics, sustainability
- The importance of ethics to:
  - The accountant, the organisation, society
- The importance of professional scepticism
- Why it is important to act ethically
- The five fundamental principles of professional ethics
- Threats to the fundamental principles
- The safeguards which can mitigate threats to the fundamental ethical principles
- Steps that can be taken to resolve ethical conflict
- The consequences of unethical behaviour.

Learners need to be able to:

- Demonstrate professional scepticism
- Identify breaches of the fundamental principles
- Identify threats to the fundamental principles
- Identify safeguards used to protect from threats to the fundamental principles
- Recommend safeguards to protect from threats to the fundamental principles
- Recommend action to take when there is ethical conflict
- Identify conflicts of interest
- Recommend actions to take when there is a conflict of interest.

3.2 **Law**

Learners need to understand:

- Money laundering offences
- The consequences for an accountant of failing to act appropriately in response to money laundering
- The protection given to accountants by protected disclosures and authorised disclosures
- The requirements for registering for anti-money laundering supervision
- How to report suspected money laundering
- The procedures that an accountant should implement to prevent and detect money laundering
- The meaning of bribery
- The consequences of bribery
- The meaning of whistleblowing
- The legal protection for whistleblowers

Learners need to be able to:

- Identify money laundering offences
- Identify consequences of money laundering
- Identify weaknesses in money laundering procedures
- Identify steps to report money laundering
- Identify bribery
- Identify when whistleblowing is appropriate

Assessment context

In the assessment, you should be prepared to identify ethical conflicts, recognise breaches of professional principles and consider appropriate safeguards. You may need to demonstrate professional scepticism and identify issues relating to money laundering, bribery or whistleblowing, applying ethical and legal requirements to real lifestyle scenarios.

Qualification context

Ethics underpins the AAT qualification, but this chapter provides you with a deeper understanding of how ethical and legal responsibilities work together in practice. This knowledge will support you when using judgement in other Level 4 units, such as Financial Accounting and Audit and Internal Controls, where professional behaviour is essential.

Business context

Ethical behaviour and legal compliance are central to maintaining trust in financial information. Recognising ethical challenges and understanding your responsibilities helps you make decisions that protect the organisation and the public. Ensuring that financial crime is prevented and reported appropriately strengthens governance and helps maintain the organisation's reputation.

Chapter overview

Understanding ethics and law in an accounting environment

- **Law and ethics**
  - Ethics and ethical values
  - The importance of ethics and its relationship with the law
  - Personal ethics
  - Business ethics
  - Professional ethics
- **Fundamental principles of ethics for accounting technicians**
  - Integrity
  - Objectivity
  - Professional competence and due care
  - Confidentiality
  - Professional behaviour
- **Threats to fundamental ethical principles**
  - Self-interest
  - Self-review
  - Advocacy
  - Familiarity
  - Intimidation
- **Safeguards for fundamental ethical principles**
  - Safeguards created by the profession and/or legislation and regulation
  - Safeguards in the work environment
- **Resolving ethical conflict and consequences of unethical behaviour**
  - The conceptual framework
- **Personal and professional qualities of an accountant**
  - Personal qualities of an accountant
  - Professional qualities of an accountant
  - Importance of professional scepticism
- **Consequences of unethical behaviour**
  - The accountant
  - The Accountancy Profession
  - Society as a whole
- **Important areas of law for accountants**
  - Money laundering, bribery and whistleblowing
- **Money laundering**
  - Money laundering process
  - Money laundering offences
  - Reporting money laundering
  - Registering for anti-money laundering supervision
  - Procedures to prevent and detect money laundering
- **Bribery**
  - Bribery offences
- **Whistleblowing**
  - Protected disclosures

Introduction

Ethics and legal compliance are central to the role of the accounting professional. Accountants are responsible for preparing, analysing and communicating financial information that is relied upon by businesses, investors and regulators. As a result, they must act with integrity and in accordance with both professional ethical standards and the law to maintain trust and support effective decision making.

This chapter explores how **ethics and the law interact** within an accounting environment. It begins by examining the distinction between legal requirements and ethical responsibilities, and how personal, business and professional ethics influence behaviour in the workplace. The chapter highlights the importance of acting ethically not only for individual reputation, but also for the credibility of organisations and confidence in the wider business environment.

You will then study the **fundamental principles of professional ethics**, including integrity, objectivity, professional competence and due care, confidentiality and professional behaviour. The chapter explains common **threats to these principles**, such as self-interest or familiarity, and the **safeguards** that can be applied at both an organisational and professional level to reduce these risks. It also outlines how ethical conflicts can be approached and resolved using a structured framework, and considers the consequences of unethical behaviour for individuals, organisations and society.

In addition, the chapter introduces key areas of **law relevant to accountants**, particularly **money laundering, bribery** and **whistleblowing**. You will develop an understanding of how financial crime can occur, the responsibilities of accountants in preventing and reporting suspicious activity, and the procedures organisations must implement to comply with legal requirements. The role of whistleblowing, including protected disclosures and legal safeguards, is also considered as part of maintaining transparency and accountability.

By combining ethical principles with legal obligations, this chapter demonstrates how accountants contribute to good governance and responsible business practice. It reinforces the importance of acting with integrity, applying professional judgement, and complying with regulations to protect both the organisation and the wider public interest.

1 Law and ethics

In this section we begin our study of law and ethics by considering the difference between laws and ethics, the different types of ethics and why they are important to accountants, business organisations and society.

1.1 Ethics and ethical values

KEY TERM

> **Ethics:** A set of moral principles that guide behaviour.
>
> **Ethical values:** Assumptions and beliefs about what constitutes 'right' and 'wrong' behaviour.

Individuals, business and organisations all can have **ethical values**, often reflecting the beliefs of the families, cultures and educational environments in which their ideas developed.

1.2 The importance of ethics and its relationship with the law

Many centuries ago, mankind discovered that the standard of living can be increased for all via **mutual co-operation**. Over time, this coexistence was formalised and regulated by the development of standards and principles, and today these are formalised in **law**.

Laws set the minimum expectations for regulating the behaviour of our society, and tend to do so by prohibiting certain actions, such as theft and murder, and punishing those who commit them.

In a fair and civilised society, higher living standards and greater co-operation are often achieved by **voluntarily exhibiting behaviour** that **exceeds the minimum requirements** laid down by law, this involves **acting ethically**. There is no legal requirement to act ethically, but individuals and organisations who act unethically often suffer negative consequences, for example an unethical organisation may find that it loses customers (and therefore revenue).

In more recent times, **sustainability** has become another important factor in people's lives. We shall study sustainability in a later chapter, but increasingly, people and business organisations are becoming concerned about the environmental and social impact of our everyday lives. In a similar way to ethics, organisations and people now have their own views, values and principles that they may follow in relation to sustainability in both a business and personal capacity.

We can therefore appreciate that the **law, ethics and sustainability** are all **interrelated**. For example:

- The law sets the minimum standard of behaviour expected by society.
- Ethics set a higher standard of behaviour expected by society than merely doing the legal minimum.
- Sustainability involves individuals and business realising the impact that they have on the world and on others and minimising and rectifying any negative impacts.
- As ethics and sustainability increase society expectations of behaviour, the law adapts. For example, there are now many environmental rules and regulations in place that did not exist before sustainability become an important global topic.
- As the law adapts to changes in society, the minimum standard of expected behaviour increases, driving changes to what society expects in an ethical and a sustainability context.

1.3 Types of ethics

Ethics and be categorised as **personal ethics**, **business ethics** and professional ethics.

1.3.1 Personal ethics

Personal ethics are the values, beliefs and principles that are important to an individual. These values, beliefs and principles help guide us in our everyday life in terms of making decisions and how we relate to others.

Personal ethics can be categorised in many ways. For example:

- **Egotists** – look to maximise their personal outcomes and look after their own needs.
- **Pluralists** – look for outcomes that benefit everyone.
- **Relativists** – look at the context of the ethical decision and are prepared to be flexible and pragmatic.
- **Absolutists** – look at the fundamental correctness of a course of activity, and thus tend to be guided by laws and regulations.
- **Consequentialists** – look at the possible consequences of a decision before deciding what to do.

The following factors can influence a person's ethics:

- **The law** – legislation sets the minimum standard of behaviour where the person lives. Knowing what the minimum standard of behaviour is will influence a person in deciding whether or not to act above this level.
- **Ethical codes** – professions often have written codes and principles that they expect their members to follow. Individuals may decide to embody these ethics in their non-work life as well.
- **Social pressure** – social pressure can change the values and views of the public (for example in regard to environmental and discrimination issues) can influence a person's ethics as they wish to feel part of a group or society.
- **Corporate culture** – corporate culture is 'the sum of all the beliefs, attitudes, norms and customs that prevail within an organisation' or 'the way we do things around here'. Organisations often try to encourage an ethical culture, and as with professional codes of ethics, individuals may embody organisational ethics in their day-to-day life as well.
- **Personal background** – an individual's gender, age, family and religious beliefs will affect their ethics.

Ethics are important to society because they raise the bar of acceptable human behaviour, improving living conditions and how people relate to each other. You only need to look back into history to see that people treated others in a way that would be totally unacceptable now. That improvement is largely down to ethics.

Activity 1: Your ethics

Think of some examples of the kinds of behaviour that you consider 'right' or 'wrong' in your personal and professional life.

1.3.2 Business ethics

A relatively recent phenomenon is the acceptance that **'good ethics can be good business'.** By this we mean that there can be a financial payback for companies that go above and beyond their minimum obligations.

Businesses may therefore develop their own unique **ethical values**, and perhaps publish them in a **Corporate Code of Conduct.** There is no set content for such codes, but many are in the form of guidelines on areas such as integrity, customer focus and honesty. These values can sometimes be seen in their corporate mission statements, objectives, internal working practices as well as the products and service that they supply.

Some organisations appoint **Ethics (or Compliance) Officers** whose role it is to oversee the application of ethical policies and be a point of contact for employees who may need help to resolve ethical dilemmas.

Business ethics is about **applying ethical principles to business problems**. When determining whether an action is right or wrong several factors should be considered:

- The consequences of the action (does the end justify the means?).
- What is the motivation for the action?
- Are there any guiding principles to follow (such as treating others as you would like to be treated?
- Are there any key values that should be followed (such as human rights)?

Where businesses are found to have acted unethically, they breach the trust that society places in them, and this can have devastating effects on their reputations and consequently, their sales.

Real life example

Some examples of ethical issues in business include:

- Avoiding tax through legal loopholes
- 'Creative accounting'
- Copying the products and designs of competitors
- Product issues such as planned obsolescence and not rectifying defects
- Using misleading marketing methods
- Issues around environmental or social impacts of operations
- Aggressive selling techniques
- Employee discrimination and unfair dismissal
- Data protection and privacy
- Insider dealing and price fixing
- Bribery and corporate hospitality
- Business intelligence and industrial spying (espionage)
- Donations to political parties to gain influence

The table below sets out the **importance** and **costs of business ethics**:

Importance of business ethics	Costs of business ethics
Attracts customers – ethics can enhance an organisation's reputation and brand.	**Increased costs** – materials from ethical sources are often more expensive.
Improves workforce effectiveness – ethics often promote good working conditions and strong teamwork that improves productivity. Anti-discrimination policies help broaden the range of employees and helps attract high-calibre staff.	**Lost business** – ethical organisations may have to turn down work from unethical customers.
Cost reduction – ethics can help minimise costs due to less wastage and less tax on polluting activities.	**Resource costs** – loss of management time due to planning and implementing ethical policies.
Risk reduction – following ethical principles helps to reduce the business risk of unethical activities.	

1.3.3 Professional ethics

Professional accountants have a leadership role in society, and as such, society expects them to behave and act in the public interest. Incidents such as the collapse of large multinational organisations have severely dented public confidence in the accounting profession, further increasing the need for clear and ethical guidelines.

We will see in a later topic how the AAT regulates the affairs of its members, but here we can consider the **importance of ethics** to **accountants** and the **accountancy profession**.

- Ethical issues may also be a **matter of law,** so need to be followed.
- The **profession is represented by each of its members**, so relies on each and every one of them to uphold certain standards.
- An accountant's ethical behaviour serves to protect the **public interest** (the common well-being to general welfare of society).
- The **consequences of unethical behaviour** impact not only on the accountant's own career, but can jeopardise the jobs of others and endanger the reputation of the whole industry.
- **Accountants** employed in the **public sector** are **duty-bound to protect taxpayers' money**.

2 Fundamental principles of ethics for accounting technicians

We shall now focus on the ethics that are most relevant to you as a student or member of the AAT, the **AAT's Code of Professional Ethics**.

You should already be very familiar with the Code because it is examinable at all levels of the qualification. Therefore, much of what we will be covering should be familiar. However, it is important that you study it carefully.

When studying this section, keep the following points in mind as they will help bring everything into focus. To behave in an ethical manner, accounting technicians should:

- Completely avoid even the appearance of **conflict of interest**
- Be **objective** and act in the **public interest**, because your responsibility is not exclusively to satisfy the needs of an individual client or employer
- Keep sensitive information **confidential** – accountants often deal with their employer's or client's most private material
- Be **straightforward** and **honest** in professional and business relationships
- Maintain **professional knowledge**, **behaviour** and **skills** at the level required by a client or employer
- Act within the **spirit** and the **letter of the law** so as not to bring the profession into disrepute
- Understand that **mere compliance** with the law or regulations may **not constitute ethical behaviour** because the law is just the minimum standard of behaviour that is tolerated – behaving ethically means doing more than the legal minimum

The table below summarises the **five fundamental ethical principles** set out in the **AAT Code of Professional Ethics** (AAT, 2017) that underpin ethical behaviour in an accounting context:

Fundamental principle	Explanation
Integrity	A member shall be 'straightforward and honest in all professional and business relationships'. They should consistently apply high moral values.
Objectivity	A member shall 'not allow bias, conflict of interest or undue influence of others to override professional or business judgements'.
Professional competence and due care	A member has a continuing duty 'to maintain professional knowledge and skill at the level required to ensure that a client or employer receives competent professional service based on current developments in practice, legislation and techniques. A member shall act diligently and in accordance with applicable and professional standards when providing professional services'.
Confidentiality	A member shall, 'in accordance with the law, respect the confidentiality of information acquired as a result of professional and business relationships and not disclose any such information to third parties without proper and specific authority, unless there is a legal or professional right or duty to disclose. Confidential information acquired as a result of professional and business relationships shall not be used for the personal advantage of the member or third parties'.
Professional behaviour	A member shall 'comply with relevant laws and regulations and avoid any conduct that discredits the profession'.

2.1 Integrity

On an everyday level, integrity involves matters such as being **open** about the limitations of your knowledge or competence, being **honest** in your relationships and carrying out your work **accurately, conscientiously and efficiently**.

2.2 Objectivity

This is a very important principle for the accounting profession because it protects the interests both of the parties directly affected by an accountant's services and of the general public (who rely on the accuracy of information and the integrity of financial systems).

Objectivity is the principle that all **professional** and **business judgements** should be made fairly:

- On the basis of an **independent** and intellectually honest appraisal of information
- **Free from all** forms of **prejudice** and **bias**
- Free from factors which might affect **impartiality**, such as pressure from a superior, financial interest in the outcome, a personal or professional relationship with one of the parties involved, or a **conflict of interest** (where you are in a position of having to choose between two conflicting outcomes – for example where one client stands to lose and another to gain by a particular disclosure you need to make)

2.3 Professional competence and due care

Accountants have an obligation to their employers and clients to know what they are doing – and to do it right!

You should understand that you must not agree to carry out a task or assignment if you do not have the **competence** to carry it out to a **satisfactory standard** – unless you are sure that you will be able to get the help and advice you need to do so. And if you discover in the course of performing a task or assignment that you lack the knowledge or competence to complete it satisfactorily, you should not continue without taking steps to get the help you need.

In addition, once you have become a member of the profession, you need to **maintain** and **develop** your **professional** and **technical competence**, to keep pace with the demands which may be made on you in your work and developments which may affect your work over time. This may mean:

- Regularly reviewing your working practices against national and international standards, codes, regulations and legislation. Are you complying with the latest requirements?
- Continually upgrading your knowledge and skills in line with developments in accounting practices, requirements and techniques – and making sure that you do not get 'rusty' in the skills you have!

Due care is a legal concept that means that, having agreed to do a task or assignment, you have an obligation to carry it out to the best of your ability, in the client's or employer's best interests, within a reasonable timescale and with proper regard for the technical and professional standards expected of you as a professional.

As someone who is knowledgeable about accountancy, you may often deal with others who have little knowledge of accounting matters. This puts you in a position of power, which must never be abused by carrying out your task or assignment in a negligent or 'careless' way.

2.4 Confidentiality

Confidentiality requires individuals to protect information from unauthorised disclosure and applies to information obtained through professional or business relationships.

Finance professionals are routinely entrusted with highly sensitive data, including financial results, budgets, salaries, pricing strategies, tax information, and future business plans. Such information must not be shared with others unless there is a legal or professional obligation to do so.

Although it is a very important fundamental principle, there are circumstances where the law **allows or requires** that confidentiality to be breached. These circumstances are described in the AAT Code of Professional Ethics (AAT, 2017) and are summarised in the table below.

Circumstance	Examples
'Disclosure is required by law, and is authorised by the client or the employer'	Providing documents or other evidence for legal proceedings Disclosure to HMRC Disclosure of actual/suspected money laundering or terrorist financing to the firm's Money Laundering Reporting Officer (MLRO) or to the National Crime Agency (NCA)
'There is a professional right or duty to disclose which is in the public interest and is not prohibited by law'	Complying with the quality review of an IFAC member body or other professional body Responding to an inquiry or investigation by the AAT or other regulatory or professional body Disclosure to protect the member's professional interests in legal proceedings Disclosure made to comply with technical standards and ethics requirements

It is vital to appreciate the importance of the fundamental principle of **confidentiality**. You need to respect the confidentiality of information acquired as a result of professional and business relationships. This means that you will not use or disclose confidential information to others, unless:

- You have **specific** and **'proper' authorisation** to do so by the client or employer
- You are **legally** or **professionally entitled** or **obliged** to do so

It is also worth being aware that personal information shared with you by clients and colleagues at work should be regarded as confidential, unless you are told otherwise: this is an important basis for trust in any working relationship.

2.5 Professional behaviour

The final fundamental principle is professional behaviour.

For example, when advertising their services, members must ensure that they are honest and truthful. They can bring the profession into disrepute by making **exaggerated claims** about services, their qualifications and experience, or if they make **disparaging references** or **unsubstantiated comparisons** to the work of others.

Applying this principle means **'being professional'**. You'll have your own ideas about what 'being professional' means. Certainly, it involves complying with the law and behaving in a way that maintains or enhances the reputation of your profession: bringing it credit – not discredit.

One key aspect of this is **courtesy**. As a professional, you should behave with courtesy and consideration towards anyone you come into contact with in the course of your work and indeed in your personal life.

It is impossible for us to overstate the importance of each of these fundamental principles – you MUST be able to recognise each of them.

3 Threats to fundamental ethical principles

The AAT Code of Ethics identifies **threats to the fundamental principles**. These threats create a risk of compromising the fundamental principles and will fall into one of the following five categories. You are expected to be mindful of them at all times. If a threat occurs, then you will be expected to deal with it by applying one of the safeguards that follow this section.

Threat	Explanation	Examples
Self-interest	'Financial or other interests will inappropriately influence the member's judgement or behaviour'	Undue fee dependence on one particular client

Threat	Explanation	Examples
Self-review	'A previous judgement needs to be re-evaluated by the member responsible for that judgement'	Tax and accountancy work carried out by the same engagement team
Advocacy	'A member promotes a position or opinion to the point that subsequent objectivity may be compromised'	Acting on behalf of an assurance client which is in litigation or dispute with a third party
Familiarity	Due to 'a close or personal relationship, a member becomes too sympathetic to the interests of others'	A senior member undertaking an assurance engagement for a number of years for the same client
Intimidation	'A member may be deterred from acting objectively by threats' (actual or perceived)	Threatened withdrawal of services by a dominant client

Activity 2: Threats

A student member of the AAT has been asked by their manager to amend a financial report that they have produced. The result of the report as it stands means that the manager will not receive a bonus. The manager has conveniently reminded the student that they will be conducting their performance appraisal in the near future.

Required

Which threat is the student AAT member facing?

	✓
Familiarity	
Self-interest	
Advocacy	
Intimidation	

4 Safeguards for fundamental ethical principles

The **AAT Code of Professional Ethics** (AAT, 2017) defines **safeguards** as **'actions or other measures that may eliminate threats or reduce them to an acceptable level'**. The Code identifies two broad categories of safeguards that you might use to reduce or eliminate the threats we have described above.

- **Safeguards** created by the **profession** and/or **legislation** and **regulation**. These include:
  - Education, training and experience, as requirements for entry into the profession
  - CPD
  - Corporate governance regulations
  - Professional standards
  - Professional or regulatory monitoring and disciplinary procedures
  - External review of financial reports, returns, communications or information produced by members

- **Safeguards** in the **work environment**, which increase the likelihood of identifying or deterring unethical behaviour, include:
  - Quality controls, and internal audits of quality controls
  - Mechanisms to empower and protect staff who raise ethical concerns ('whistleblowers')
  - Involvement of, or consultation with, independent third parties (eg non-executive directors or regulatory bodies)
  - Rotation of personnel to avoid excessive familiarity and opportunities for collusion in fraud
  - Opportunities to discuss ethical dilemmas (eg with an ethics officer, committee or forum)

5 Resolving ethical conflict and the consequences of unethical behaviour

It is impossible to give guidelines on every possible situation that may arise in the course of your work which conflicts with the fundamental ethical principles.

The **AAT Code of Professional Ethics** (AAT, 2017) therefore sets out a basic **problem-solving procedure,** which you can use in any situation, to give yourself the best chance of complying with the principles. This procedure forms the 'conceptual framework' which requires the following:

- **Identify** where there may be a **threat** to a fundamental principle.
- **Evaluate** the threat: how significant is it?
- For any significant threat **apply safeguards** that will eliminate the threat or reduce it to an acceptable level (so that compliance with the fundamental principle is not compromised).
- If safeguards cannot be applied, **decline** or **discontinue** the specific action or professional service involved or, where necessary, resign from the client (if you are a member in practice) or the employing organisation (if you are a member in business).

Identifying and evaluating threats and the application of safeguards all require the application of an accountant's **professional judgement**. Although professional judgement is a **personal view,** based on an accountant's training and experience, it is expected that all members of the profession would act in a broadly similar way given the same circumstances.

Assessment focus point

Whilst assessments may test knowledge of ethics (including the fundamental principles, threats and safeguards) it is more likely that you will be required to apply these aspects to a scenario given to you. Therefore, it is important to be able to identify when an ethical dilemma exists and to understand what you need to do to respond to it appropriately.

6 Personal and professional qualities of an accountant

Aside from the need to promote ethical behaviour. Accountants should also demonstrate personal and professional qualities.

Personal qualities of an accountant

(a) **Reliability** – you should be trustworthy and dependable

(b) **Responsibility** – you should take ownership for your actions and decisions

(c) **Respect** – you should develop constructive relationships, and this involves listening and understanding other people's points of view

(d) **Timeliness** – being able to work within agreed timeframes

(e) **Courtesy** – conducting yourself with courtesy, consideration and good manners

Professional qualities of an accountant

(a) **Independence of mind** – being able to act with objectivity and freedom from bias, and **independenceof appearance** – would a reasonable and objective third party consider you to be independent of mind?

(b) **Professional scepticism** – questioning the veracity of information provided to you; challenging management assertions and being alert to misstatements due to error or fraud. Professional development helps individuals apply the right amount of scepticism depending on the circumstances

(c) **Accountability** – being responsible and answerable for your actions

(d) **Social responsibility** – the individual as a stakeholder in society must behave with integrity, courtesy, respect and due care

Of the professional qualities of an accountant, **professional scepticism** is one of the most important as you will need to apply it regularly in your work.

Whenever you **receive information** you should be considering whether it is **accurate** and **reliable,** where it has come from and any motivations of the person who provided you with it. This quality is crucial in your role as it will help you **avoid providing inaccurate** or **misleading information** to others. It is particularly important when looking at **automatically generated information**, such as from an organisation's information systems or **Artificial Intelligence.** Information produced by such systems should be carefully reviewed by a professional to ensure it can be relied upon.

7 Consequences of unethical behaviour

When considering the **consequences of unethical behaviour** it is sensible to start by considering the relationship between the AAT Code of Ethics and the law.

The AAT Code is a **law of the institute,** and therefore any breach of the Code can give rise to disciplinary action. However, the Code is not part of national law, and therefore will not automatically give rise to civil or criminal actions, though these *could* follow if the breach is also against the law.

When considering how the AAT's Code, the law and contracts interact it is important to remember that the **law overrides everything.** As a student or member of the AAT your secondary obligation is to the AAT's Code, even if it may cause a breach of your employment, or other contract. Contracts such as an employment contract, or ones entered into in the course of business are entered into voluntarily. This means that you always have a choice not to comply with a contractual obligation and you should do so if by complying with it you would break the law or be in breach of the AAT's Code.

Real life example

Frank is an AAT member working for Lennox Ltd. Frank has been put in charge of finalising construction contracts for a new warehouse, and uses this position to negotiate some 'kickbacks' for himself with certain suppliers. In one instance, Frank agreed to accept a tender for building materials that was 10% higher than an equivalent quote of £500,000 on the understanding that Frank would receive an undeclared cash payment of half of the difference.

In this instance, Frank has breached the AAT code with respect to objectivity, integrity, confidentiality and professional behaviour. He therefore faces disciplinary action from AAT that could result in his expulsion from the institute. In addition to this, Frank's actions could lead to a criminal prosecution under the Bribery Act (see later in this chapter), so he faces prison and/or a fine; the undeclared payments may also lead to action from the tax authorities. Finally, Lennox Ltd would be justified in dismissing Frank, and could take civil action to recover any amounts they have overpaid as a result of the unlawful awarding of contracts.

The illustration above highlights the potential interaction between the AAT Code, the national law and an individual's employment contract.

The consequences of unethical behaviour can be far reaching and will impact the accountant concerned, the accountancy profession and society in general.

7.1 The Accountant

There are several consequences for an accountant who does not behave ethically or follow the AAT's Code:

- Ethical issues may be a matter of **law and regulation.** You are expected to know and apply the **civil and criminal law** of the country in which you live and work – as a basic minimum requirement for good practice. The AAT Code is based on the **laws effective in the UK**, with which members are expected to comply as a **minimum requirement.** (It is sometimes said that 'the law is a floor': the lowest acceptable level of behaviour required to preserve the public interest and individual rights.)
- The **AAT** (like other professional bodies) requires its members to conduct themselves, and provide services to clients, according to certain professional and ethical standards (which means more than merely acting 'professionally'). It does this, in part, to **maintain its own reputation and standing** – but this is also of benefit to its members and to the accounting profession as a whole.
- Professional and ethical behaviour protects the **public interest.** The accountancy profession sees itself as having duties to society as a whole – in addition to its specific obligations to employers and clients.
- **Disciplinary action** may be taken **by the AAT** against members who have acted in breach of the code (fines, reprimands, warnings, or suspension or expulsion from membership).
- Organisations my suffer **fines** or **reputational damage** because of an employee's unethical behaviour, for example where laws or regulations were breached.
- **Disciplinary action** may be taken **by the AAT member's employer** for unethical behaviour which may result in them losing their job.

7.2 The Accountancy Profession

Accountants have a **high degree of trust** placed on them by society. Therefore, any high-profile or repeated breaches can have severe consequences for the whole profession. These may include:

- Loss of reputation
- Reduced employability of accountants
- Pressure by outside bodies to tighten up regulations and penalties
- Government intervention if it is thought the profession is incapable of self-regulation
- Accountancy bodies losing their 'chartered' status.

7.3 Society as a whole

Given that **society relies upon the work of accountants** to assess the profitability of organisations and their liability for tax, there are **consequences for the wider society** of unethical behaviour.

- The work of all accountants would be called into question.
- Unethical companies would eventually fail as they would lose public confidence.
- The financial markets would be affected if investors could not rely on audit reports and financial statements.
- The tax authorities may question tax computations, affecting the amount of tax collected.
- Criminals may gravitate towards the profession to make money from fraud or other financial crime.
- Commercial organisations would not function if they were unable to rely on their accountants' work.

8 Important areas of law for accountants

Having studied ethics and the importance of ethics to the accountancy profession, we shall now look at three important areas of law for accountants; money laundering, bribery and whistleblowing.

8.1 Money laundering

KEY TERM

Money laundering: Attempts to make the proceeds of crime appear respectable. It covers any activity by which the apparent source and ownership of money representing the proceeds of income are changed so that the money appears to have been obtained legitimately.

Money laundering is a **crime** that is **against the interests of the state**, and it is associated with drug and people trafficking in particular, and with organised crime in general.

8.2 Money laundering process

The **money laundering process** usually involves three phases:

Stages in money laundering process	Explanation
Placement	The initial disposal of the proceeds of the initial illegal activity into apparently legitimate business activity or property
Layering	The transfer of monies from business to business, or place to place, to conceal the original source
Integration	Having been layered, the money has the appearance of legitimate funds

8.3 Money laundering offences

There are **three categories of criminal offences** in the **Proceeds of Crime Act 2002** (TSO, 2002). However, the offence of money laundering is also controlled by **Money Laundering Regulations.**

Offence	Explanation
Laundering	The acquisition, possession or use of the proceeds of criminal conduct, or assisting another to retain the proceeds of criminal conduct and concealing, disguising, converting, transferring or removing criminal property. There is no de minimis limit, so an offence may be committed in respect only of £1. Penalty: 14 years' imprisonment and/or a fine. Assets may also be confiscated.
Failure to report	Failure to disclose knowledge or suspicion of money laundering ('suspicion' is more than mere speculation, but falls short of proof or knowledge). Penalty: Five years' imprisonment and/or a fine.
Tipping off	Disclosing information to any person if disclosure may prejudice an investigation into drug trafficking, drug money laundering, terrorist-related activities, or laundering the proceeds of criminal conduct. Penalty: Five years' imprisonment and/or a fine.

The **key offences for an accountant** to be aware of is **failure to report** and **tipping off**. They mean that accountants have a legal duty to report money laundering and to avoid disclosing information regarding the reporting of money laundering to anyone if it would impact an investigation.

Activity 3: Money laundering

Which of the following is not a UK offence relating to money laundering?

	✓
Concealing the proceeds of criminal activity	
Telling a client that you have heard that they have been reported on suspicion of money laundering	
Failure to pay sufficient tax	
Failing to report suspicion of money laundering	

8.4 Protected disclosures and authorised disclosures

Under the **Proceeds of Crime Act 2002**, accountants are given important legal protections when they report suspected money laundering.

A **protected disclosure** shields an accountant from any legal or contractual restrictions — such as confidentiality – that would normally prevent them from passing information to the authorities. This protection applies whether the accountant works within the regulated sector or voluntarily reports suspicions arising in their professional work.

An **authorised disclosure** protects an accountant from committing a money-laundering offence when they suspect they may already be involved in handling criminal property. By making a timely disclosure to the appropriate authority they gain a legal defence and avoid liability for continuing a potentially criminal transaction. These disclosures are treated as lawful and do not breach confidentiality obligations.

Together, these protections encourage accountants to report concerns without fear of breaching client confidentiality or exposing themselves to criminal liability, supporting the wider UK system for detecting and preventing money laundering.

8.5 Reporting money laundering

Where a person suspects money laundering has taken place, they must disclose this to a **nominated officer** (sometimes called a **money laundering reporting officer** or MLRO) within their organisation. The nominated officer is responsible for assessing the information, making any necessary enquiries, and deciding whether a **Suspicious Activity Report** (SAR) should be submitted to the authorities.

If the nominated officer decides the **suspicion is justified,** they submit a SAR to the UK Financial Intelligence Unit. When a disclosure is made correctly, it becomes a **protected disclosure**.

If someone suspects money laundering but cannot access a nominated officer, they may alternatively directly report their suspicions to the **National Crime Agency** by making a Suspicious Activity Report themselves.

8.6 Registering for anti-money laundering supervision (AML)

In the UK, **certain businesses** and **professionals** – including accountants, tax advisers and other accountancy service providers – must register with an approved supervisory authority before carrying out work that falls within the scope of the Money Laundering Regulations.

These regulations require firms to be **formally supervised** to ensure they meet their obligations around customer due diligence, record keeping, internal controls, risk assessment and reporting of suspicious activity.

Firms must register with the **correct supervisory body**, or a **recognised professional body** such as the AAT. Registration generally involves providing details about the business, its services and ownership, and putting in place AML policies, procedures and controls in line with the Money Laundering Regulations. These include appointing a nominated officer, training staff, and establishing systems to recognise and report suspicious activity. Failing to register, when required, is a breach of the regulations and can lead to civil penalties or criminal sanctions.

8.7 Procedures to prevent and detect money laundering

Accountants in the UK must have **robust anti-money laundering (AML) procedures** in place to comply with the **Money Laundering Regulations** and the **Proceeds of Crime Act 2002**.

These procedures begin with conducting a **risk assessment** of the business and its clients. Firms must implement **strong customer due diligence measures, maintain appropriate record-keeping**, and **monitor ongoing business relationships** for unusual or suspicious activity.

Firms must also establish **internal controls,** including appointing a **nominated officer** to receive and assess internal reports of suspicious activity as well as internal checks on so that one employee's work is reviewed by another member of staff. They should also **train staff** to recognise indicators of money laundering and ensuring procedures are followed consistently are essential for detecting suspicious behaviour early and meeting legal obligations.

These procedures work together to help accountants identify risks, comply with reporting duties, and protect their firms from being misused for criminal purposes.

9 Bribery

The **Bribery Act 2010** (TSO, 2010) brought together, and is intended to simplify, the previous law on bribery and corruption which was contained in both common law and statute.

The maximum **penalty** for bribery under the Act is **ten years' imprisonment** and/or an **unlimited fine**.

9.1 Bribery offences

The **Bribery Act** created **four main offences,** the first three of which are committed by **individuals** while the fourth is a **corporate** offence.

In terms of the offence, a **relevant function** or **activity** includes any function of **a public nature** or any **activity connected with business** or **carried out in the course of employment**.

It applies to individuals who perform that function or activity from a **position of trust** or are otherwise expected to perform it in **good faith** or **impartially**.

The **offences** are set out in the following table:

Offence	Explanation
Bribing another person	This offence is committed where a person offers, promises or gives financial or other advantages to another person with the intention of inducing that person to perform improperly a relevant function or activity, or to reward them for such improper performance. It does not matter whether or not the person being bribed is the same person as the one who would usually perform the function or whether the offer is made directly or via a third party.
Being bribed	This offence is committed where a person requests or accepts a financial or other advantage improperly, or as a reward for improper performance of a relevant function or activity, or intending that improper performance should result. It does not matter whether the advantage is received direct or through a third party. The offence also applies if a person receives a benefit on behalf of another person.

Offence	Explanation
Bribing a foreign public official	This offence is similar to that of bribing another person, but is committed where the bribe is offered to a foreign public official (FPO). An FPO is any individual who holds a legislative, administrative or judicial position of any kind outside the UK, or who exercises a public function outside the UK, or who is an official or agent of a public international organisation.
Corporate failure to prevent bribery	The offence of corporate failure to prevent bribery is committed by an organisation that fails to prevent a bribery offence being committed by a person who performs services for it in any capacity – such as an agent, employee or subsidiary. Under the Act, an organisation includes companies and partnerships based in the UK or doing business in the UK.

10 Whistleblowing

KEY TERM

Whistleblowing: is the name commonly given to workers making a disclosure of wrongdoing (usually) by their employer.

The relevant legislation is the **Public Interest Disclosure Act 1998** (PIDA).

The protection is afforded to workers generally (and not just to 'employees') and there is no requirement as to age or length of service.

In order to receive protection under PIDA, the worker must:

- Reveal the right type of information (a qualifying disclosure)
- Reveal the information to the right person in the right way (a protected disclosure)

Real life example

Goode vs Marks & Spencer – Mr Goode was an employee of 25 years of Marks and Spencer (M&S). He was sacked for gross misconduct after passing an internal email outlining proposals to reduce redundancy benefits by up to 25% to a newspaper. Mr Goode's suspension sparked a public row that proved embarrassing for both the retailer and the group's chief executive.

Goode claimed he passed on the internal memo outlining proposals to cut redundancy benefits because he felt that the internal consultation process that the company was undertaking about the plans was a 'sham'.

Mr Goode's plea that his sacking was a breach of human rights was rejected as insufficient grounds for making the disclosure. Crucial to the case was the fact that M&S's plans were only in outline at the time and no decision on implementation had been taken.

A disclosure is a qualifying disclosure if, in the reasonable belief of the worker making it, the information disclosed tends to show one or more of the following:

(a) That a criminal offence has been committed, is being committed or is likely to be committed
(b) That a person or company has failed, is failing or is likely to fail with any legal obligation to which he is subject
(c) That a miscarriage of justice has occurred, is occurring or is likely to occur
(d) That the health and safety of an individual has been, is being or is likely to be endangered
(e) That the environment has been, is being or is likely to be damaged
(f) That information tending to show any matter falling within these categories has been, is being or is likely to be deliberately concealed

A disclosure is **protected disclosure** if:

(a) It was made in good faith
(b) There is reasonable belief that it is substantially true
(c) There is reasonable belief that the disclosure is being made to the right person (such as any appropriate internal person, a legal adviser, a government minister or professional body).

Disclosures to government ministers are only appropriate for public sector workers. The information can also be revealed to the media but stricter rules apply.

Workers who have made a protected disclosure have the right not to suffer a detriment, such as lack of promotion, lack of training or opportunity, unjustified disciplinary action, pay issues or failure to renew contracts as a result of having made a protected disclosure.

An 'employee' who is dismissed or selected for redundancy for having made a protected disclosure shall be regarded as having been automatically unfairly dismissed. Any gagging clause in conflict with the Act will be void.

Activity 4: Whistleblowing

In some cases, a worker may intend to disclose wrongdoing by his employer to someone outside the workplace; for example, the police. In such cases, the disclosure will be protected by the Public Interest Disclosure Act 1998 if it is reasonable in all the circumstances and is not made for personal gain. In addition, the worker will need to satisfy one of several other criteria in order to receive the protection of the Act (assuming that the matter disclosed is a qualifying disclosure within the Act).

Required

Which one of the following is NOT one of those criteria and will not, therefore, afford the statutory protection?

	✓
The fact that he had already raised the matter internally	
Reasonably believing that a cover-up was likely and there was no prescribed person to whom disclosure could be made	
Reasonably believing that he would be victimised if he raised the matter internally	
The fact that the matter was of a serious criminal nature	

Assessment focus point

Money laundering, bribery and whistleblowing are key areas of law that affect accountants. Assessments could easily test your knowledge of the laws related to these issues as well as your understanding of how to respond to them.

Chapter summary

- Individuals, business and organisations all can have **ethical values**, often reflecting the beliefs of the families, cultures and educational environments in which their ideas developed.
- **Laws set the minimum expectations for regulating the behaviour of our society**, and tend to do so by prohibiting certain actions, such as theft and murder, and punishing those who commit them.
- In a fair and civilised society, higher living standards and greater co-operation are often achieved by **voluntarily exhibiting behaviour** that **exceeds the minimum requirements** laid down by law, this involves **acting ethically**.
- **Personal ethics** are the values, beliefs and principles that are important to an individual. These values, beliefs and principles help guide us in our everyday life in terms of making decisions and how we relate to others.
- **Business ethics** is about **applying ethical principles to business problems.**
- **Professional accountants** have a leadership role in society, and as such, society expects them to behave and act in the public interest.
- The **Five Fundamental Ethical Principles** of the AAT's Code of Ethics are: Integrity, objectivity, professional competence and due care, confidentiality and professional behaviour.
- The AAT Code of Ethics identifies **threats to the fundamental principles.** These threats create a risk of compromising the fundamental principles and will fall into one of the following five categories.
- The **AAT Code of Professional Ethics** defines **safeguards** as **'actions or other measures that may eliminate threats or reduce them to an acceptable level'**. The Code identifies two broad categories of safeguards that you might use to reduce or eliminate the ethical threats.
- The AAT Code of Professional Ethics sets out a **basic problem-solving procedure**, which can be used in any situation, to help comply with the ethical principles. This procedure forms the 'conceptual framework'.
- The **consequences of unethical behaviour** can be far reaching and will impact the accountant concerned, the accountancy profession and society in general.
- **Money laundering** is an attempt to make the proceeds of crime appear respectable. It covers any activity by which the apparent source and ownership of money representing the proceeds of income are changed so that the money appears to have been obtained legitimately.
- Money laundering stages are **placement**, **layering** and **integration**.
- Money laundering offences are **laundering, failure to report** and **tipping off**. Accountants must be careful to comply with the rules on reporting suspicions of money laundering and avoid tipping off.
- A **protected disclosure** shields an accountant from any legal or contractual restrictions – such as confidentiality – that would normally prevent them from passing information to the authorities.
- An **authorised disclosure** protects an accountant from committing a money-laundering offence when they suspect they may already be involved in handling criminal property.
- Where a person suspects money laundering has taken place, they must disclose this to a **nominated officer** (sometimes called a **money laundering reporting officer** or MLRO) within their organisation. The nominated officer is responsible for assessing the information, making any necessary enquiries, and deciding whether a **Suspicious Activity Report** (SAR) should be submitted to the authorities.
- In the UK, **certain businesses** and **professionals** – including accountants, tax advisers and other accountancy service providers – must register with an approved supervisory authority before carrying out work that falls within the scope of the Money Laundering Regulations.
- **Accountants** in the UK must have **robust anti-money laundering (AML) procedures** in place to comply with the **Money Laundering Regulations** and the **Proceeds of Crime Act 2002.**
- The **Bribery Act** created **four main offences,** the first three of which are committed by **individuals** while the fourth is a **corporate** offence.

- **Whistleblowing** is the name commonly given to workers making a disclosure of wrongdoing (usually) by their employer.
- Workers who make a **protected disclosure** have the right not to suffer a detriment, such as lack of promotion, lack of training or opportunity, unjustified disciplinary action, pay issues or failure to renew contracts as a result of having made a protected disclosure.

Activity answers

Activity 1: Your ethics

This is personal to you, so that you begin to think about your own assumptions and beliefs about what kinds of behaviour are 'OK' and 'not OK'. Some of these may be in line with the ethical values of the AAT and the accounting profession (such as being honest, telling the truth, being fair and working hard) and some may not be (such as using your work position for the benefit of family members, or offering gifts as a smoother of business relationships and negotiations). In a way, these instances – where your values differ from the professional standards – are more useful information: you know where your 'blind spots' are, and where you may have to modify your assumptions and habits.

Activity 2: Threats

The correct answer is:

	✓
Familiarity	
Self-interest	
Advocacy	
Intimidation	✓

Pressure from the manager and the reminder about the student's performance appraisal indicates an intimidation threat.

Activity 3: Money laundering

The correct answer is:

	✓
Concealing the proceeds of criminal activity	
Telling a client that you have heard that they have been reported on suspicion of money laundering	
Failure to pay sufficient tax	✓
Failing to report suspicion of money laundering	

Failure to pay sufficient tax is not a money laundering offence in itself. But if there is deliberate tax evasion, the transfer or hiding of the proceeds of this criminal offence would constitute money laundering.

Activity 4: Whistleblowing

The correct answer is:

	✓
The fact that he had already raised the matter internally	
Reasonably believing that a cover-up was likely and there was no prescribed person to whom disclosure could be made	
Reasonably believing that he would be victimised if he raised the matter internally	
The fact that the matter was of a serious criminal nature	✓

The other options are incorrect. However, the seriousness of the matter is one of the factors considered in determining whether a disclosure made was reasonable in all the circumstances.

Test your learning

1 Respond to the following by selecting the appropriate option.

Required

Only individuals can have 'ethical values'.

	✓
True	
False	

2 **A client asks you a technical question about accounting standards which you are not sure you are able to answer correctly. 'You are supposed to be an accountant, aren't you?' says the client. 'I need an answer now.' What should you do first?**

	✓
Say that you will get back to him when you have looked up the answer.	
Give him the contact details of a friend in your firm who knows all about accounting standards.	
Clarify the limits of your expertise with the client.	

3 **An AAT member who acts in a straightforward and honest manner is said to be following the fundamental principle of integrity.**

	✓
True	
False	

4 Which of the following applies in the event of a valid whistleblowing?

Required

	✓
The worker is entitled to keep his job	
The employer is liable to a fine	
The worker will be deemed automatically unfairly dismissed if they lose their job	
The employer must make a written apology to the worker	

5 **Which of the following best reflects an accountant's legal responsibility under UK money-laundering legislation?**

	✓
Only report suspicious activity if the client gives permission.	
Wait until full evidence of criminal activity is confirmed before taking any action.	
Share suspicions with colleagues informally before deciding whether to report.	
Submit an internal report to the firm's nominated officer whenever there is knowledge or suspicion of money laundering.	

4 Understanding the effective use of data in business

Learning outcomes

4.1 Recording data

Learners need to understand:

- The methods of data collection
  - Primary/secondary, internal/external, sample/whole population
- The process of cleaning data
  - Identify omissions, error detection, rectification
- Types of errors in data:
  - Systematic errors, random errors, negligent errors

Learners need to be able to:

- Identify the most appropriate method of data collection
- Identify situations where there may be errors in data
- Identify errors in data
- Identify the impact of errors in data
- Clean data

4.2 Using data and data protection

Learners need to understand:

- The benefits that data analytics can provide to an organisation:
  - Speed, decision making, risk reduction, efficiency
- The different types of data analytics:
  - Descriptive, diagnostic, predictive, prescriptive
- The principles of data protection
- The risks to data and organisational operations caused by:
  - Cyberattacks (phishing, malware, denial of service, ransomware), unauthorised access, physical loss of equipment, data issued in error, data amended or deleted in error
- The importance of protecting commercially sensitive information
- The impact of data protection breaches on the individual and business
- The impact of Artificial Intelligence (AI):
  - Data collection, data use, ethics, sustainability, legal compliance

Learners need to be able to:

- Identify the principles of data protection
- Recommend how to protect data
- Identify the potential consequences of not protecting data

4.3 **Presenting data**

Learners need to understand:

- The value of a narrative in addition to data and visualisations
- That interpretation of visualisations can vary
- The issues arising with the use of:
  - Spreadsheets, social media, other digital applications
- Data bias
- The difference between correlation and causation
- Ethical issues in relation to:
  - Data visualisation, data use

Learners need to be able to:

- Interpret visualisations
- Identify ways to reduce data bias
- Distinguish between correlation and causation

Assessment context

During the assessment, you may be expected to identify suitable methods of data collection, detect errors or omissions, and consider the impact of poor quality information. You should be prepared to demonstrate an understanding of data analytics, data protection principles and cyber risks. You might also need to interpret data presented visually and distinguish between correlation and causation.

Qualification context

Accurate data is vital across the Level 4 qualification, especially in areas such as Management Accounting and Audit and Internal Controls. This chapter helps you develop the skills to work with data confidently, evaluate its quality and understand how data protection and digital risks affect business information.

Business context

Organisations depend on reliable data to make informed decisions. Poor data quality can lead to incorrect conclusions, operational disruption and regulatory breaches. By understanding how to collect, clean, analyse and interpret data effectively, you can help ensure information is used responsibly and that commercially sensitive data is protected.

Chapter overview

Understanding the effective use of data in business

Recording data

- Primary and secondary sources of information
- Valid, accurate and reliable information
- Internal and external information
- Sampling and whole population data
- Data errors
- Cleaning data

Data and data protection

- Data analytics
- Types of data analytics
- Data protection principles
- Risks to data
- Protecting commercially sensitive information
- Impact of data protection breaches on individuals and businesses
- Artificial intelligence (AI)

Presenting data

- Data visualisation
- Spreadsheets, social media and digital applications
- Data bias, correlation and causation and ethical issues relating to data

Introduction

Data plays an increasingly important role in modern business, supporting organisations in making informed decisions, improving efficiency and identifying opportunities for growth. However, data is only valuable when it is accurate, reliable, properly analysed and used responsibly. For accounting professionals, the ability to work effectively with data is essential to providing meaningful insights and supporting organisational performance.

This chapter explores how data is **recorded, analysed, protected and presented** within a business context. It begins by examining the different methods of **data collection**, including primary and secondary sources, and the importance of ensuring that data is valid, accurate and reliable. The chapter also considers the need for **data cleaning**, identifying errors such as omissions or inaccuracies, and understanding how these can affect the quality of information used in decision making.

The chapter then moves on to how data is used within organisations through **data analytics**, highlighting its role in improving speed, efficiency and risk management. You will explore different types of analytics—descriptive, diagnostic, predictive and prescriptive—and how they support business decisions. Alongside this, the importance of **data protection** is emphasised, including the principles organisations must follow, the risks posed by cyberattacks and human error, and the potential consequences of data breaches. The growing impact of **artificial intelligence (AI)** is also introduced, particularly in relation to data use, ethics and compliance.

Finally, the chapter considers how data is **presented and interpreted**, focusing on the use of visualisations and the importance of providing a clear narrative alongside data. It highlights challenges such as **data bias**, differences in interpretation, and the need to distinguish between **correlation** and **causation**. Ethical considerations in the use and presentation of data are also addressed, reinforcing the responsibility of accounting professionals to communicate information clearly and accurately.

By linking data quality, analysis, protection and communication, this chapter demonstrates how effective data use supports better decision making and organisational success. It highlights the critical role accountants play in ensuring that data is not only technically accurate, but also used responsibly and communicated in a way that adds real value to the business.

1 Recording data

In this section we begin by considering what information is and where it comes from. Accurate and reliable information is critical to business decisions so we will also study the various types of data errors and how they can be detected and rectified.

1.1 Methods of data collection

1.1.1 Primary and secondary sources of information

KEY TERM

Primary information: Information collected specifically for a particular purpose.

Secondary information: Information collected for some other purpose than what it is being used for.

A **primary source of information** is as close as you can get to the origin of an item of information. Accountants often collect primary information when they carry out investigations. A good example would be the establishment of the direct cost of a product. This might be carried out by analysing materials invoices and wages costs over a representative period.

Advantages of primary information	Disadvantages of primary information
The investigator knows where the information has come from	Cost – it can be very expensive to collect primary information

Advantages of primary information	Disadvantages of primary information
The investigator is aware of any inadequacies or limitations in the information	Time – it can be very time consuming to collect the information

A **secondary source of information** provides 'second-hand' information, in other words the person or organisation using the information is not the one who originally collected it. For example, a company might consult trade journals and the internet for information about a particular industry before deciding to set up business in that industry. This decision will be based on secondary information.

Secondary information sources may be satisfactory in certain situations, or they may be the only convenient means of obtaining an item of information. It is essential that there is good reason to believe that the secondary information used is **valid, accurate** and **reliable**.

Advantages of secondary information	Disadvantages of secondary information
They are cheaply available.	There may be inadequacies or limitations of the information.
There is potentially a large quantity available.	The information may be out of date.
It is usually quicker to obtain secondary information than primary information.	There may be no relevant information available.
Secondary information can be useful for analysing the past, eg patterns.	The information may be incorrect (especially if found through unverified sources).

1.1.2 Valid, accurate and reliable information

KEY TERM

Valid information: Information that is relevant, strongly associated, and appropriate to the purpose it is being used for.

Invalid information: The direct opposite of valid information. It is not relevant or strongly associated with the purpose it is being put to and therefore it is not appropriate to use it.

There may be nothing wrong with information labelled as invalid, it just means that the information is not appropriate for a particular use.

For example, a company's bank statement would be valid information if you wanted to perform a bank reconciliation at the statement's date, but it would not be valid if you wanted to use the same bank statement to perform a bank reconciliation for a date two months later.

When choosing what information to use, you must be mindful of the **specific purpose** you are using it for. Consider all the sources of information available to you and make sure the information selected is valid for that purpose.

KEY TERM

Accurate information: Information that is factually and numerically correct. In other words, the information is supported by evidence and all the numbers and any calculations work mathematically.

The accuracy of information is affected by its **sensitivity to change**. Information which starts off as accurate may become inaccurate over time. For example, a company's statement of financial position is an accurate snapshot of the company's finances on a particular day. However, by the time the financial statements are published the company's financial situation will have changed and it will no longer accurately represent the company's current financial position.

KEY TERM

Reliable information: Information that can be trusted, depended upon and can be considered genuine and authentic.

Reliability is often determined by the **source** that provided or collected the information. Some sources are more reliable than others. For example, information about a country's economic performance is likely to be more reliable if it comes from an official government source rather than from a blog on the internet.

1.1.3 Using information from different sources

An organisation may obtain information from internal or external sources. **Internal information** is created by the organisation itself; **external information** is produced outside of the organisation. The following table provides some examples of each.

Internal sources of information	External sources of information
Accounting records and reports	Government statistics
Payroll system	Trade journals
Production records	Credit reference agencies
Time sheets	Marketing agencies
Customer account records	Industry bodies

Sometimes you may find that you have **more than one valid source** of information available to you. There are several **benefits** from using **information** from **more than one source.**

- One source may corroborate information from another source, increasing the overall reliability of the information.
- It reduces the risk that information might be biased, as bias in one information source may be compensated by another information source.
- It provides a wider perspective of the overall picture created by the information.
- Accuracy of information from one source can be confirmed by another source.
- Having multiple sources of information should make it easier to find valid information.

Whenever you are producing information it is important to **recognise** (or refer to) the **sources** that you used. This means identifying where you obtained the information from. Recognition could be simply a link to a web page, the title and page number of a publication or a full academic reference.

Importance of recognising information sources
Allows the reader to refer back to the original source documents for more information or to verify your information
Helps the reader decide whether your information is valid, accurate and reliable for their purposes
Demonstrates professional standards and presentation of your work
If the information is being published outside of the organisation, then references are required to comply with rules on copyright

Activity 1: Valid sources of information

Identify the valid source of information for each of the following business activities using the picklist.

Business activity	Information source
Calculating employee pay based on the number of hours worked	▼
Forecasting the country's inflation rate	▼
Costing activities in the production process	▼
Researching the price of a competitor's products	▼
Identifying the amount of tax to be paid to HMRC on employee salaries	▼

Picklist

- Company website
- Government statistics
- Payroll system
- Production records
- Time sheets

1.1.4 Sampling and whole population data

When a business collects data, it must decide whether to **gather information from every member** of the population it is interested in, or whether to **collect data from only a subset** (sample) of that population. The choice affects the cost, accuracy and usefulness of the data.

Whole population data

KEY TERM

Whole population data: Also called a census, **whole population data collection** involves collecting information from every individual, item or event within the group being studied.

The organisation designs a data-collection process that captures information from **everyone or everything in scope**. This may be done automatically (eg EPOS tills recording every sale) or manually (eg staff checking each product in a warehouse).

Examples include:

- A retailer analysing all customer transactions for a month.
- A manufacturer reviewing every machine output for quality control.

Benefits	Risks
High accuracy No estimation is needed because the full population is measured.	Time consuming and costly Large populations require significant resources to measure in full.
Useful for small populations When numbers are low, it may be easier to gather all data than create a meaningful sample.	Data overload Businesses may struggle to store, process or interpret very large datasets.

Benefits	Risks
Removes sampling bias (see later) Decisions can be based on complete information.	Collecting errors at scale If a measurement method is flawed, the error affects the entire dataset.

Sampling

KEY TERM

> **Sampling:** Sampling involves collecting data from a smaller, representative subset of the full population. The results are then used to estimate or predict what is likely to be true for the whole group.

Businesses design a sampling method that aims to represent the wider population accurately. Common techniques include:

- **Random sampling** – Every member has an equal chance of being selected.
- **System sampling** – Every member has an equal chance of being selected.
- **Stratified sampling** – Dividing the population into sub groups (eg age, region) and sampling within each group.

The organisation then collects data from the chosen sample and analyses results using statistical methods.

Benefits	Risks
Lower cost and faster results Especially useful for large populations.	Sampling error (see later) Results may differ from the true population values, especially with poorly chosen samples.
Reduced data handling requirements Easier to process and analyse than full datasets.	Risk of bias (see later) If the sample does not accurately represent the population (eg surveying only certain customer types), findings may be misleading.
Enables testing Allows pilot studies or preliminary research before full-scale data collection.	Less useful for small populations Sampling may miss important variations when numbers are low.

Choice between sampling methods

In practice, businesses **select the method** based on:

- Population size
- Cost and time constraints
- Required accuracy
- Availability and reliability of data sources

For example:

- A supermarket analysing loyalty-card sales may use whole-population data because it is automatically recorded.
- A company conducting customer satisfaction research may use sampling, as surveying every customer would be impractical.

1.2 Data errors

When businesses collect and process data, errors can arise that reduce its accuracy and reliability. Understanding the different types of errors helps organisations identify the cause and choose appropriate solutions. The main types of data errors include systematic errors, random errors, negligent errors, and several other important categories.

1.2.1 Systematic errors

KEY TERM

> **Systematic errors:** Systematic errors occur when data is consistently incorrect in the same direction or pattern. They stem from flaws in the data collection process, measuring tools, or procedures.

Systematic errors are often **predictable** and **repeatable**, introduce bias into results and are often hidden unless the system is analysed carefully

Examples of systematic errors:

- A faulty factory sensor consistently recording temperature 2°C too high
- A spreadsheet formula that miscalculates totals
- Staff consistently entering dates in the wrong format (DD/MM/YYYY instead of MM/DD/YYYY)

Systematic errors can significantly distort business decisions because they affect the entire dataset in a uniform way, making results appear reliable even though they are incorrect.

1.2.2 Random errors

KEY TERM

> **Random errors:** Random errors are unexpected, unpredictable variations in data that occur without a consistent pattern. They often result from temporary conditions or human variation.

Random errors tend to be **irregular** and **inconsistent in nature,** difficult to eliminate completely, but are less problematic with larger sample sizes as they do not affect all data items, unlike systematic errors.

Examples of random errors:

- Fluctuations in timing when employees manually time how long processes take to complete
- Minor input errors such as keying "101" instead of "110" once
- Variations in factory sensor readings caused by environmental conditions

Random errors can reduce the precision of results and create noise in data analysis. However, they usually average out over time and do not create systematic bias.

1.2.3 Negligent errors

KEY TERM

> **Negligent errors:** Negligent errors arise from carelessness or failure to follow proper procedures during data entry, collection, or processing.

Negligent errors tend to be **human-caused** and **preventable** through **training** and **quality control**. They are often inconsistent but they are avoidable.

Examples of negligent errors

- Employees not manually entering all data on an online form due to rushing
- Entering data into the wrong system or wrong customer record
- Misreading labels, instructions or units

These errors reduce data reliability and can be costly if they occur in financial or operational systems. They also indicate weaknesses in staff training or process design.

1.2.4 Other types of data errors

The table below sets out other important types of error to be aware of.

Type of error	Explanation
Measurement errors	Occur when tools, devices or systems used to capture data give inaccurate results. Examples: Mis calibrated weighing scales and incorrectly configured software settings. Measurement errors lead to incorrect values that may affect areas such as inventory control, production quality, or performance reporting.
Transcription errors	Arise when data is incorrectly copied from one place to another. Examples: Mis-typing numbers when transferring information from a paper form to a digital system, losing digits when copying invoice numbers and mistakenly duplicating or omitting entries. Transcription errors are particularly problematic for financial data or identifiers used for tracking items.
Processing errors	Happen when data is manipulated or processed incorrectly by formulas, software, or human intervention. Examples: Incorrect spreadsheet formulas, data processing scripts that exclude certain records and sorting data improperly, leading to misalignment of values. Processing errors can cause major reporting inaccuracies, especially in automated systems.
Duplication errors	Occur when the same record appears multiple times in a dataset. Examples: A customer appearing twice with slightly different name spellings and duplicate transactions after a system error. Duplication errors cause issues such as inflated totals, inaccurate counts, and confusion in customer/supplier management.
Outlier and anomaly errors	Extreme values that fall outside what would normally be expected. These can be legitimate but may also indicate an error. Examples: A product quantity of "5000" instead of "50", negative stock levels and a delivery time of "0 minutes". Outlier and anomaly errors may distort averages, charts and forecasting models.

1.3 Cleaning data

KEY TERM

> **Data cleansing:** The process of identifying and correcting errors, gaps and inconsistencies within a dataset to ensure that the information a business uses is accurate, complete, reliable and fit for analysis.

Clean data reduces the risk of poor decision making and improves the quality of insights gained from business information systems. Clean and accurate data supports:

- Reliable performance analysis
- Better forecasting and planning
- More accurate financial and operational reporting
- Improved customer and supplier management
- Stronger compliance with regulations and audit requirements

The data cleansing process consists of three main stages.

1.3.1 Identifying omissions

Omissions occur when required data is missing, incomplete or only partially recorded. For example, a customer record with no email address, a sales invoice missing the quantity sold and a production log with gaps in machine readings.

Missing data can distort calculations, hinder reporting and reduce the effectiveness of forecasting or decision-making. Therefore, it is important for organisations to look for ways to minimise them occurring.

The following tests and checks can **help identify omissions**:

- **Completeness checks** – automated tests to identify data fields that are blank.
- **Validation rules** – tests that are built into the data entry process that, for example, highlight missing mandatory information.
- **Comparison checks** – comparing related datasets to spot missing items. For example, to identify an order without a matching delivery note.

1.3.2 Detecting errors

Errors arise when **data has been entered incorrectly** or **inconsistently**. For example, typographical errors (eg "1,0000" instead of "1,000"), incorrect codes or categories used in data entry, duplicated records and values occurring that are outside of expected ranges (eg negative stock levels).

Incorrect data can lead to misleading results, inaccurate reports, and operational issues such as sending goods to the wrong address or misreporting financial figures.

The following **procedures** can help a business detect errors in its data:

- **Validation rules** – if not built into the data entry process can be applied to data that is in the system.
- **Automated checks for duplicates** – checking that the system does not hold the same sales invoice twice for example.
- **Comparing data to known, reliable sources** – such as checking supplier codes against an approved supplier list.
- **Reviewing outliers or unusual patterns** – software can be set up to flag anything unusual and to produce a report containing them for human review.

1.3.3 Rectifying problems

Once omissions or errors are identified, businesses need to **correct them** and **prevent similar issues** occurring in future.

Methods of rectification include:

- **Completing missing information** by referring back to original documents, contacting customers/suppliers, or pulling from other internal systems.

- **Correcting incorrect** values, for example by fixing spelling errors, adjusting quantities, amending codes.
- **Removing or merging duplicates.**
- **Standardising data** formats, such as by using consistent date formats or postcode formatting.
- **Updating validation rules** in data entry systems to prevent repeated mistakes

When rectifying errors it is **good practice** to:

- **Record** how and why changes were made
- Keep **audit trails** for accountability
- **Train staff** on proper data entry procedures
- Use **automated tools** where possible to reduce manual effort

Assessment focus point

Be prepared to be tested on your knowledge of the various types of data and information and how they are collected. Questions may also test your understanding of the importance of creating accurate and reliable data by identifying errors and knowing how to cleanse them.

2 Data and data protection

In the previous section we looked at how data is collected and processed into a form that will help a business create accurate and reliable information. In this section we focus on how organisations analysis this data and the issue surrounding data processing and storage.

2.1 Data analytics

KEY TERM

Data analytics: The collection, management and analysis of large data sets with the objective of discovering useful information that an organisation can use for decision making.

To have value to an organisation, data needs to have meaning. **Data analytics** creates this meaning by assembling, filtering, sorting, highlighting and finally presenting the data in useful forms.

Some key impacts that data analytics can bring to an organisation are summarised below.

Area of impact	Description
Decision making	Large volumes of data can be analysed in real-time to help managers make better decisions that improve profitability.
Marketing	Analysis can be performed on customer data so that the organisation can customise its marketing approach to individuals or customer groups.
Risk	Analytics can provide management with a better understanding of the risks that the organisation faces, particularly in the business environment.
Product development	Analysis of the organisation's market and customer needs can help to identify opportunities to develop new products and services.
Knowledge	Analytics can create and enhance knowledge. For example, customer buying patterns or trends in supplier costs, which the business did not know before, might be identified.

Area of impact	Description
Performance management	Deeper levels of understanding of the organisation's performance may identify previously unknown causes for poor performance that can be rectified.

According to CIMA (2020), business consultants **McKinsey** have identified **six benefits that effective data analytics** bring to an organisation.

Benefit	Description
Fresh insight and understanding	Intelligent use of data can reveal patterns and insight into how a business operates and identify previously unknown issues.
Improved performance (efficiency)	The processing of data and the creation of relevant management information in real time can result in improvements to operations, decision making and resource utilisation.
Segmentation and customisation of markets	The needs and wants of customer groups can be increasingly refined, leading to better personalisation and customisation of products and services.
Fast decision making (speed)	Real-time processing of data results in faster decisions and advantage over the competition.
Innovation	Existing products can be improved through the organisation better understanding the aspects of the product that customers value the most. New products can also be developed.
Risk management and reduction	Data analytics can support all aspects of the risk management process.

2.2 Types of data analytics

Businesses use **data analytics to extract meaning** from data and support better decision-making. There are four main types of data analytics (descriptive, diagnostic, predictive and prescriptive) and each answers a different question and provides different levels of insight.

Type of data analytics	Explanation
Descriptive analytics	Summarises and presents what has happened in the past by organising historical data into clear, understandable information. It focuses on identifying patterns and trends using tools such as totals, averages, charts and dashboards. It does not explain why something happened – it simply describes the outcomes. For example: A retailer analyses last quarter's sales figures to see which products sold most frequently and how overall revenue has changed month by month.

Type of data analytics	Explanation
Diagnostic analytics	Investigates why something happened by examining relationships, anomalies and causes within the data. It goes deeper than description, looking for underlying drivers through techniques such as drill down analysis, correlation analysis, and data comparisons. The aim is to explain the reasons behind past performance. For example: After noticing a fall in customer satisfaction scores, a company analyses feedback comments, store level data and staffing records to identify that long waiting times were the main cause.
Predictive analytics	Uses historical data and statistical models to forecast what is likely to happen in the future. This type of analytics applies methods such as trend forecasting, regression analysis and machine learning models to estimate future outcomes. While not perfect, predictions help businesses anticipate opportunities and risks. For example: A subscription service analyses past customer behaviour to predict which users are at high risk of cancelling, allowing the company to take retention actions.
Prescriptive analytics	Recommends what actions should be taken to achieve the best possible outcome. It builds on predictive models by suggesting decisions, strategies or interventions based on potential scenarios. Prescriptive analytics often uses optimisation techniques and advanced algorithms to recommend the most effective course of action. For example: A delivery company uses route optimisation software that analyses traffic patterns, fuel costs and delivery schedules to recommend the most efficient routes for drivers each day.

2.3 Data protection principles

Once organisations have collected data, they must ensure that how they process, store and use that data complies with any applicable national laws. In the UK, this is the **Data Protection Act 2018** (TSO, 2018). This this law enacted the EU's **General Data Protection Regulation** (GDPR) that was introduced in 2018.

The GDPR (and therefore the Data Protection Act) set out the following **six principles** to protect data that concern individuals (not businesses).

Principle	Description
Lawfulness, fairness and transparency	Data can only be held if there are valid grounds to do so. Data can only be used fairly and with clarity, openness and honesty in how the data is used from the start.

Principle	Description
Purpose limitation	Individuals must be made aware of the purpose of recording the data from the time it is first collected. This purpose must be specified, explicit and legitimate. Should data need to be used for a different purpose in future, then consent from the individual must be obtained unless there are legal grounds to do otherwise.
Data minimisation	Data held must be adequate (sufficient to fulfil the purpose), relevant (connected to the purpose for holding it) and not excessive (the minimum needed to fulfil the purpose).
Accuracy	Data held must be accurate and not misleading. Reasonable steps should be taken to ensure there are no inaccuracies. Any data that is found to be inaccurate or misleading must be corrected.
Storage limitation	Data must not be held for longer than is needed for the purpose it was collected and processed. There should be a justifiable data retention policy that can be justified. Data that is not needed must be deleted or anonymised.
Integrity and confidentiality (security)	Appropriate security measures regarding the risks that might arise in connection with the data must be taken.

The **Data Protection Act 2018** establishes the following eight rights for individuals under UK law. Other countries may have established similar rights.

Right	Description
To be informed	Individuals must be informed about how their personal data is collected and used. Information that must be shared includes (for example) the purposes that their data is used for, what the retention period is, and who the information is shared with. Individuals must be given this information at the time that their personal data is collected, or within a month if the data was collected from another source.
Access	Individuals have the right to request information held about them either verbally or in writing. The requested information must be supplied within one month, and (in most circumstances) there should be no charge for it.
Rectification	Individuals can request inaccurate or misleading information held about them to be rectified. Incomplete information must be made complete. The request can be made verbally or in writing and it must be completed within one month. Only in limited circumstances can the request be refused.
Erasure	This is known as the right 'to be forgotten'. Individuals may request information held about them be destroyed. This request can be made verbally or in writing. This right only applies in certain circumstances and a reply must be sent to the data subject within one month.
Restrict processing	Individuals can have restrictions placed on the processing of their data or have it suppressed altogether. The data can still be held, but it must not be processed. They can request the restriction verbally or in writing. The right only applies in certain circumstances and the individual must be given a response within one month.

Right	Description
Data portability	Individuals can request to be sent the data held about them so they can reuse it in a different service. For example, data held by an online banking app can be requested and transferred to another app that can make use of it (such as a money manager type app).
To object	Individuals can object to the processing of their data. Where the data is used in connection with direct marketing, there is an absolute right to object. Where the data is used for other purposes, this right can be refused if there is a compelling reason to do so. The objection can be made verbally or in writing and a reply must be sent to the data subject within one month.
Automated decision making and profiling	Other data protection rights are granted to individuals where data held about them is used to make automated decisions about them, or where data evaluation about them is automated, for example where decisions are made by bank computer systems as to whether or not to lend money to an individual. The uses of data in this way are limited and the individual must be given information about the processing. They also have the right to request human intervention or to challenge decisions made following such processing.

Activity 2: Providing information

You have been asked for the following information. Should each item be provided?

Required

Indicate whether you would provide the information or, if not, indicate the reason why.

	Yes – provide information ✓	No – personal information ✓	No – confidential information ✓
A colleague asks for the email address of a customer so they can contact them about an order they placed			
The partner of a customer asks you for the details of what their partner ordered recently.			
The receptionist at head office has requested the names of people due to visit you today.			

2.4 Risks to data

An organisation's data and information is a highly valuable resource. Not only does it contain important information for business decision making, but it also contains data and other files that are necessary for information and other systems to operate. Any loss or damage to this data will therefore not only impact decisions, but also whether or not day-to-day business operations can continue.

Real life example

In 2025, a cyberattack on car manufacturer Jaguar Land Rover (JLR) became the UK's costliest cyber security incident at £1.9bn when car production was halted for 5 weeks.
https://www.bbc.co.uk/news/articles/cy9pdld4y81o

Not all risks to data are electronic and we shall also consider other risks to data later in the section.

2.4.1 Cyber-risk, cyberattack and cybersecurity

KEY TERM

Cyber-risk: A term that covers a number of organisational risks which are possible consequences of a cyberattack. Cyber-risks include financial losses, reputational damage and operational disruption.

Cyberattacks: Deliberate attempts to damage an organisation by using the Internet to take advantage of poor security controls and system integrity.

Cybersecurity: The protection of computer systems from the risk of cyberattack through the use of hardware and software security procedures and controls.

2.4.2 Key cyber-risks

The **main risks** to an organisation that cyberattacks may bring include:

(a) **Financial loss** – the risk that the organisation will lose money, either through having funds directly stolen, but also the cost of repairing the damage caused by a cyberattack (including the payment of fines if IT controls are deemed not sufficient to protect customer data).

(b) **Damage to reputation** – the risk that customers and suppliers may view the organisation as a potentially risky partner to deal with.

(c) **Loss of trust by customers** – customers may fear that they will be affected by a cyberattack themselves through the organisation in future.

(d) **Disruption to the organisation** – the risk that operations will either be reduced or entirely cease due to the attack. For example, an attack may affect the organisation's financial systems that allow it to pay suppliers or collect money from customers.

2.4.3 Types of cyberattack

The table below contains examples of the **common types** of cyberattack.

Type of cyberattack	Description
Phishing	The cyberattacker sends emails to the victim which appear to be from a trusted source, for example a bank. The emails request the victim sends back security information (such as usernames and passwords) and personal details and uses them to steal funds from the victim.
Pharming	The cyberattacker targets an organisation's website by automatically redirecting visitors from the organisation's website to a bogus website. The intention is to collect data to commit fraud and is similar to phishing.
Hacking	The cyberattacker uses specialist software and other tools to gain unauthorised access to an organisation's computer system and take administrative control. Such control allows them to view and copy system records, as well as amend or delete information that they find. Some hackers may try to stop the system working altogether.

Type of cyberattack	Description
Distributed denial of service (DDoS) attack	The cyberattacker attempts to disrupt an organisation's online activities by preventing people from accessing the organisation's website. Botnets (large numbers of individual computers which have been taken over without the user knowing) are instructed to overwhelm the organisation's website with a wave of internet traffic so that the system is unable to handle it and may cause it to crash.
Webcam manager	The cyberattacker uses software to take control of the user's webcam.
File hijacker/ransomware	The cyberattacker gains access to the user's system to hijack their files and hold them to ransom
Keylogging	The cyberattacker plants software onto the user's computer to record what the user types onto their keyboard. The objective is to learn passwords and user details to gain access to confidential information.
Screenshot manager	The cyberattacker obtains information from the victim by installing software onto the user's computer to enable screenshots of the user's computer screen to be taken. Like other cyberattacks, the purpose can be to steal information, funds, or may even be to perform corporate espionage.
Ad clicker	The cyberattacker directs the victim's computer to a bogus website by encouraging them to click on a specific link contained in online advertising.
Malware	Any software designed to harm, exploit, or infiltrate computers, networks, or data. Common types include viruses, worms, ransomware, spyware, and trojans. A Trojan is a software program that masquerades as a desirable application, eg a virus checker, which the victim is happy to download and install. Malware can steal information, damage files, lock you out of your system, or allow attackers to gain control of your device

2.4.4 Cybersecurity methods

The table below contains some **common cybersecurity methods** used by organisations.

Cybersecurity method	Description
Access control	These are physical and network procedures to restrict access to a system.
Boundary firewalls and internet gateways	Firewalls and internet gateways are software protection that intercept data being transmitted in and out of a system.
Malware and virus protection	Malware protection software prevents installation and removes suspicious programs (such as Trojans) and viruses from a system.
Patch management	This is a system procedure rather than a hardware or software solution. The organisation should ensure that the latest software updates are installed on the system when available.

Cybersecurity method	Description
Secure configuration	The organisation should have a policy which states that systems should be set up with cybersecurity as a priority.

Activity 3: Cybersecurity

Explain how a distributed denial of service (DDoS) attack is conducted.

2.4.5 Other risks to data

As explained earlier, **not all risks to data are electronic**. Other risks include:

- **Physical loss** or damage to equipment. For example, laptops being stolen or damaged due to fire or escape of water.
- **Accidental damage** to systems and files. Where authorised users access systems and accidently delete or amend files which causes damage to them.
- **Distributing data**. The accidental sending of confidential information to those not authorised to see it. For example, the attaching a confidential document to an email which is sent to a large distribution list.
- **Unauthorised access** - access to data and information by those not authorised to see it. Such unauthorised users may interfere with, or maliciously damage or distribute data and physical equipment.

2.4.6 Secure storage of data and information

To prevent such risks to data most organisations have policies and procedures covering **data security** such as:

- The **non-removal** of data and equipment from the premises
- The frequent **backing-up** of computerised data, and the storage of backups separately from the original data, so that there are safe copies in case of systems failure, data corruption or fire
- The use of anti-virus software, firewalls and other **protective tools** on all computers, to prevent malicious corruption and theft of data

- The use of **passwords** to restrict access to computer systems or files (often with additional policies regarding the complexity and regular change of passwords) to prevent unauthorised users from obtaining, amending or deleting them
- The use of **authorisations** to control access to security-coded paper-based files
- The non-divulging of passwords, security codes and other **data security measures** to other parties

2.5 Protecting commercially sensitive information

Businesses routinely handle information that gives them an **advantage** in the market. When this information could be exploited by competitors, misused by external parties, or cause harm to the business if disclosed, it is known as commercially sensitive information.

2.5.1 What is commercially sensitive information?

Commercially sensitive information is any data that, if shared without permission, could damage the organisation's competitive position, undermine negotiations or business relationships, reduce profit or market share or lead to legal or regulatory issues.

Examples of commercially sensitive information

Example	Description
Pricing strategies	Planned price changes, discount structures, or tender pricing.
Product development information	Designs, prototypes, formulas, and research findings.
Customer and supplier data	Customer lists, purchasing behaviours, contract terms and supplier pricing.
Financial plans and forecasts	Budget projections, investment plans and upcoming acquisitions.
Operational processes	Manufacturing methods, unique technologies or internal systems.
Marketing plans	Advertising campaigns, launch dates or competitive intelligence.

2.5.2 Risks and consequences of poor protection

Failing to protect commercially sensitive information can create significant risks for a business. Key consequences include:

Consequences	Explanation
Loss of competitive advantage	Competitors gaining access to strategic plans, product designs or pricing strategies can replicate ideas, undercut prices or neutralise the organisation's strengths. This may lead to reduced market share or lower profitability.
Financial loss	Leaked tender prices or contract details may weaken future negotiations and result in less favourable deals. Loss of intellectual property can also lead to costly legal disputes.

Consequences	Explanation
Damage to reputation and trust	Customers, suppliers and partners expect businesses to handle information responsibly. A breach can reduce confidence, harm relationships and make third parties reluctant to share important data.
Legal and regulatory consequences	Some commercially sensitive information, particularly when linked to personal or contractual data, may be protected under laws such as confidentiality agreements, intellectual property rights or data protection regulations. Breaches may result in fines, legal action or regulatory scrutiny.
Operational disruption	Unauthorised access to internal processes or systems can lead to fraud, sabotage, or system vulnerabilities being exploited.

2.6 Impact of data protection breaches on individuals and businesses

When personal or confidential business data is accessed, stolen or disclosed without authorisation, the consequences can be serious. Data protection breaches damage trust, create financial risks and may lead to legal or regulatory action. Understanding the potential impacts helps organisations appreciate the importance of strong data management practices.

2.6.1 Impact on individuals

For any **individual whose data security is breached** there are numerous impacts.

Impact	Explanation
Financial loss and fraud	Personal information such as bank details, addresses or login credentials can be used for identity theft or fraudulent purchases. Victims may face financial loss or long periods spent resolving fraud issues.
Loss of privacy	A breach can expose sensitive information (eg medical data, contact details or purchasing habits). This can make individuals feel vulnerable, embarrassed or unsafe.
Emotional distress	Victims often experience worry, anxiety or stress when their data has been compromised. This can affect wellbeing, especially where highly personal information is involved.
Risk of targeted scams	Leaked information can be used to create convincing phishing attacks or impersonation scams. Individuals become more vulnerable to further exploitation.

2.6.2 Impact on businesses

Businesses who fail to keep their data secure also face a number of impacts. Many of them have already been discussed, but are summarised here with others.

Impact	Explanation
Financial penalties and legal consequences	Under data protection laws such as the GDPR and Data Protection Act 2018, organisations may face substantial fines for failing to safeguard personal data. They may also be required to compensate affected individuals.
Reputational damage	Breaches undermine customer trust. Negative publicity may lead to customers choosing competitors, harming sales and long term brand reputation.
Operational disruption	Investigating a breach takes time and resources. Systems may need to be shut down or repaired, causing downtime, reduced productivity and additional costs.
Loss of intellectual property or commercial information	If confidential business data is accessed – such as product designs, pricing models or strategic plans – it may weaken competitive advantage and affect future performance.
Increased compliance and security costs	After a breach, businesses often need to invest in improved security systems, staff training and ongoing monitoring. These additional costs can strain budgets.

2.7 Artificial intelligence (AI)

As well as data analytics, another important recent technological development is that of **artificial intelligence (AI)**. Software such as Chat GPT and Co-Pilot, as well as others have put the power of artificial intelligence within reach of anyone that has access to a computer or other technology. The rapid expansion in the use of AI has itself created several impacts.

KEY TERM

Artificial intelligence (AI): The development of computer systems that can perform tasks normally requiring human intelligence. These tasks include recognising patterns, learning from data, making decisions and solving problems. In business, AI supports automation, analysis, forecasting and improved decision making.

AI has impacted key areas of data management and business practice

2.7.1 Data Collection

AI significantly **increases the volume**, **speed** and **accuracy** of data collection.

- **Automated data capture:** AI tools can collect information from sensors, customer interactions, online behaviour and operational systems without manual input.
- **Real time monitoring:** AI systems track activity continuously, providing up to date information for decision making.
- **Improved accuracy:** Machine learning models can identify anomalies or errors during data capture, helping reduce manual mistakes.

For example, retailers use AI-powered systems to track customer movements in stores, collect purchasing behaviour, and adjust product placement based on observed patterns.

2.7.2 Data Use

AI greatly enhances the way **data is analysed**, **interpreted** and **applied** within organisations.

- **Advanced analytics:** AI speeds up complex analysis, enabling businesses to uncover patterns and insights that would be difficult to detect manually.

- **Faster decision making:** Automated systems can analyse large datasets instantly, supporting timely business actions.
- **Personalisation:** AI enables tailored recommendations, marketing messages or services based on individual behaviours.

For example, streaming services use AI to analyse viewing habits and recommend personalised content to millions of users.

2.7.3 Ethics

As AI becomes more widely used, **ethical considerations** become increasingly important.

Key ethical concerns include:

- **Bias and fairness:** AI models can unintentionally reflect or reinforce biases found in the data used to train them. We shall study data bias later.
- **Transparency:** Some AI systems operate as "black boxes," making decisions that are hard to explain or justify.
- **Human oversight:** Over-reliance on AI may reduce human judgement, leading to decisions made solely by algorithms.
- **Job displacement:** Increased automation can affect employment patterns and create ethical concerns for workforce planning.

For example, an AI recruitment tool trained on historical hiring data may favour candidates who resemble past hires, unintentionally discriminating against other groups.

2.7.4 Sustainability

AI can both support and challenge **sustainability** efforts (we shall be studying sustainability in a later chapter).

Positive impacts	Negative considerations:
Operational efficiency: AI optimises energy usage, reduces waste and improves resource management.	**Energy use of AI systems**: Large AI models require significant computing power, which increases energy demand if not managed responsibly.
Smart logistics: AI reduces fuel consumption by improving delivery routes and supply chain planning.	**Electronic waste**: Increased reliance on advanced hardware may contribute to e waste if equipment is not recycled properly.
Environmental monitoring: AI technologies analyse climate data, predict changes and support environmental protection.	

2.7.5 Legal Compliance

The use of AI requires organisations to carefully manage regulatory and legal responsibilities.

- **Data protection laws:** AI systems that process personal data must comply with regulations such as GDPR, including rules on consent, transparency and data minimisation.
- **Accountability:** Organisations must ensure they can explain how AI driven decisions are made, especially when they affect individuals.
- **Data accuracy:** Legal requirements demand that businesses keep data accurate, relevant and up to date – something AI must support rather than undermine.
- **AI-specific legislation:** Governments are introducing new regulations focused on safe use of AI, algorithmic transparency and risk management.

For example, if an AI system makes decisions about lending or credit scoring, the business must demonstrate that the process is fair, transparent and compliant with consumer protection laws.

Assessment focus point

Assessments could test many aspects relating to data and its protection. Questions may examine your knowledge of the types of data analytics, identify the data protection principles and make recommendations on how to protect data from the many risks to it. You may also be examined on the consequences of not protecting data.

3 Presenting data

So far in this chapter we have looked at the sources of data, how it is recorded and analysed, the risks to data security and the importance of data protection. This this section we now focus on how data and information is presented to the user.

3.1 Data visualisation

The **sheer volume of data** and **information** that businesses generate creates a risk that recipients of information get caught up in minutiae and **lose sight of the big picture**. The concept of **data visualisation**, is an especially useful way of presenting a wealth of information without it being overwhelming to the use.

KEY TERM

Data visualisation: The presentation of data in a pictorial or graphical format which is easier for recipients to process than detailed written data.

Examples of **data visualisation** include:

- **Bar charts** – commonly used to compare quantities (eg exam results by subject).
- **Line graphs** – useful for showing changes over time (eg monthly sales or temperature trends).
- **Pie charts** – show how a whole is divided into parts (eg percentage of sales by product category).
- **Scatter graphs** – show relationships between two variables (eg hours studied vs. exam marks).
- **Dashboards** – used in apps and websites to show metrics such as steps walked, screen time or spending activity (see below).

These tools help communicate key information quickly and effectively.

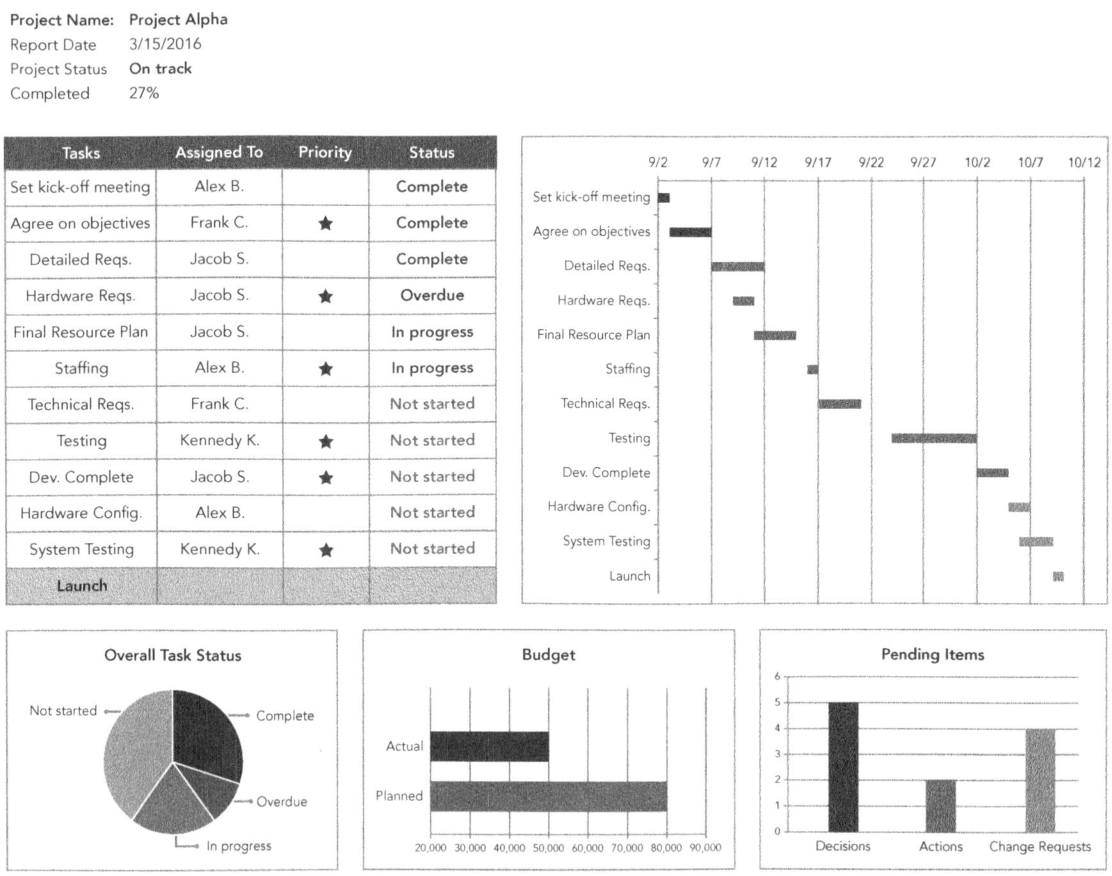

Figure 4.1: Example dashboard (Smartsheet, 2019)

Tufte (2001) identifies four ways in which data visualisation can support users of information. It can:

- **Enhance communication** – given a large number of diverse users within an organisation communication is crucial. Before visualisations, updates may have been conducted as written or verbal reports, but now data visualisation allows for key messages to be communicated clearly and succinctly. For example, **project managers** can be provided with **project dashboards** that enable users to track key metrics in a concise manner. The dashboard may include a measure of progress, milestones approaching or passed and project spending.
- **Boost collaboration** – data visualisation allows teams to work more effectively together. Processes that would be cumbersome to explain verbally can be presented and developed visually.
- **Improve clarity** – data visualisation is often based on **real-time project management software**. This means that stakeholders can track projects more closely and understand changes as they happen rather than having to wait for a written report from someone else.
- **Interactive** – data visualisation is an **interactive experience**. Instead of users being the passive recipients of a standard report, there is an opportunity for them to create their own bespoke dashboard and to drill down into areas of particular interest to them.

3.1.1 Importance of narrative

While charts and graphs are important, visualisation alone is not enough. Data needs to be accompanied by a **clear narrative** that explains what the visual is showing and why it matters.

Narrative:

- **Provides context**: Viewers need to know the background of the data – when it was collected, what it measures and why it's relevant.
- **Guides interpretation**: Narrative highlights the key messages or insights that the visual aims to show.

- **Links to decision making**: A simple explanation can turn a chart into meaningful business guidance (eg "Sales dipped in March due to supply issues – action is needed to improve stock availability").
- **Supports accessibility**: Not all readers interpret charts easily; narrative ensures everyone can understand the key points.

Without narrative, even strong visualisations can be misunderstood or ignored due to variations in interpretation between users.

3.1.2 Variation in interpreting visualisations

Visualisations are helpful, but **people can interpret them differently**, depending on their background knowledge, expectations or focus.

For example:

- A **line graph** showing sales rising might be seen as positive by one person, while another might notice the slowing rate of growth.
- A **pie chart** showing 40% market share could be viewed as impressive or as a sign that 60% belongs to competitors.
- A **bar chart** showing declining customer complaints might be interpreted as improvement – but could also reflect fewer customers overall.

This variation in interpretation demonstrates why narrative is essential: it helps align understanding and ensures the data leads to consistent, informed decisions.

3.2 Spreadsheets, social media and digital applications

Modern organisations rely heavily on **digital tools** to collect, analyse, and present data. While these tools can improve efficiency and decision making, they also introduce risks. Poorly managed digital data can lead to errors, misinterpretation, and reputational or financial damage. Of particular interest to accountants are spreadsheets, social media and other types of digital application.

3.2.1 Issues with spreadsheets

As we saw in Chapter 2, a **spreadsheet** is essentially an **electronic piece of paper** divided into **rows** and **columns** with a built-in pencil, eraser and calculator. It provides an easy way of performing numerical calculations and presenting information.

Below is a spreadsheet processing **budgeted sales figures** for three geographical areas for the first quarter of the year.

	A	B	C	D	E
1	BUDGETED SALES FIGURES				
2		Jan	Feb	Mar	Total
3		£'000	£'000	£'000	£'000
4	North	2,431	3,001	2,189	7,621
5	South	6,532	5,826	6,124	18,482
6	West	895	432	596	1,923
7	Total	9,858	9,259	8,909	28,026

Spreadsheets have many uses, both for accounting and for other purposes. It is perfectly possible, for example, to create proforma **statements of financial position** and **statements of comprehensive income** on a spreadsheet, or set up the notes for financial accounts, like the non-current assets note.

Spreadsheets are widely used because they are flexible, low cost and familiar. However, they are also one of the most common sources of data errors in organisations.

The table below sets out some reasons why spreadsheet data may be inaccurate.

Issue and examples	Explanation
Human input errors • Mistyped numbers or text • Copy and paste mistakes • Deleting or overwriting cells accidentally	Even small mistakes can create major inaccuracies because formulas depend on precise inputs.
Incorrect or broken formulas • Using the wrong formula for a calculation • Formulas referencing the wrong cells • Out of date formulas not updated as data changes	One incorrect formula can affect entire sheets, summaries, and reports.
Lack of version control • Multiple people saving their own versions • Confusion about which file is "final" • Changes made without tracking who updated what	This can result in inconsistent or outdated data being used in decision making.
Poor spreadsheet design • Complex, unstructured layouts • Hidden cells or columns • No labels, documentation or clear structure	This makes errors hard to spot and spreadsheets difficult for others to understand or review.
Overreliance on spreadsheets • Using spreadsheets as databases	Using spreadsheets for tasks they are not designed for – such as handling very large datasets or multi user editing – can lead to crashes, corruption, or missing data.

Real life example

In England, Public Health England (PHE) used Microsoft Excel spreadsheets to collate COVID-19 test results sent from laboratories. Between 25 September and 2 October 2020, 15,841 positive COVID-19 cases were not reported in official figures due to a spreadsheet error.
https://www.bbc.co.uk/news/technology-54423988

3.2.2 Issues with social media

The success of **social media sites** such as X, Facebook and Instagram has resulted in many businesses and individuals having somewhere where they can **share information** with others. Such sites allow users and organisations to **interact** in several ways:

- Posting a **status update** contain information about what the user has been doing or thoughts they have on particular issues
- **Sharing media** such as photos, music and videos
- **Sharing links** to websites and news reports
- **Sharing posts** containing all the above that other users have made
- Sending **direct messages** privately to other users

Although social media communications can benefit an organisation (such as free advertising as users share posts and media created by the business) this means of communication has several **potential negative impacts** as well.

Many of these impacts are the same as the **consequences of inappropriate sharing of information** generally.

(a) **Loss of confidential information**. Employees may be privy to confidential or sensitive information which, if made public, could cause their employer to lose competitive advantage, for example trade secrets about a new product or plans to acquire a competitor. Such information would spread very quickly across a social network if released accidentally or deliberately.

(b) **System damage**. Social media applications could be a cover for viruses or other malicious software which may be downloaded into the employee's or organisation's system through use of the social network.

(c) **Identity theft**. Much of the information posted on social networks, such as birthdays, location, addresses and phone numbers, is of use to identity thieves who pose as their victims to obtain money or goods. Individuals should ideally not post such information online, or if they do, ensure only those they trust can see it.

(d) **Deliberate damage to reputation**. Organisations and users must protect their social network accounts from hackers or unauthorised individuals who may attempt to gain access to their profile to ruin their reputation, for example, by making obscene comments about others.

(e) **Damage to reputation due to negligent or inappropriate behaviour**. Social media greys the border between work and professional life and an individual's personal life. Employees may inadvertently damage the reputation of their organisation by posting activities or thoughts that impact their employer. For example, posting images of inappropriate behaviour whilst in work uniform or making unprofessional comments about rival organisations or their own customers.

Data and information generated by social media can provide insights into customer opinions, trends and brand image. However, **data gathered** from social media can be unreliable or misleading.

Issue	Explanation
Quality and accuracy of information	Content posted online may be: • biased • exaggerated • incorrect or deliberately misleading Businesses must verify information before relying on it.
Non representative samples	Social media users do not represent the entire customer base. Data may be skewed towards particular age groups, interests or behaviours.
Volume and noise	Large quantities of unstructured data can make it difficult to identify what is relevant. High "noise levels" can hide meaningful information.
Risk of misinterpretation	Sentiment analysis tools may misread context, humour or sarcasm, leading to incorrect conclusions.
Reputational risk	Sharing inaccurate or misleading information on social media can quickly damage a business's image due to the public and fast moving nature of these platforms.

3.2.3 Issues with other digital applications

Businesses use many **digital applications,** such as customer relationship management (CRM) systems, cloud tools, project management apps, automated data collection platforms and day-to-day office tools such as word processing software. These bring additional risks.

Issue	Explanation
Data integration problems	Different systems may store data in incompatible formats. When combined, this can lead to inconsistencies or duplicated data.
System errors or glitches	Software bugs or updates can cause incorrect calculations, missing records or corrupted files.
Security and access issues	We have already seen that: • weak passwords • poor access controls • lost devices Can all lead to unauthorised access or data loss.
Overreliance on automation	Automated tools are only as good as their configuration. A wrongly set rule or workflow can systematically produce incorrect outputs.
Lack of user training	If employees do not fully understand how an application works, they may input data incorrectly, misuse features or draw wrong conclusions from outputs.

3.3 Data bias, correlation and causation and ethical issues relating to data

We conclude this chapter by looking at other areas that are important to consider when understanding data and information. These are **data bias**, **correlation** and **causation** and **ethics**.

3.3.1 Data bias

KEY TERM

Data bias: Data bias occurs when the information collected, analysed or presented does not accurately represent the real situation, leading to misleading or unfair conclusions. Bias can arise unintentionally through poor data collection, incorrect sampling, flawed assumptions or human judgement.

Biased data reduces reliability, risks incorrect decision making and can lead to unethical or discriminatory outcomes. Below are the most **common types of bias** relevant to business and data analytics.

Type of data bias	Explanation and example
Sampling Bias	Occurs when the sample used for analysis does not represent the entire population. A survey about shopping habits completed only by online customers excludes those who shop in store, leading to distorted results.

Type of data bias	Explanation and example
Selection Bias	Introduced when certain groups are more likely to be selected for analysis than others. A business evaluating staff performance using data only from employees who completed optional training may assume training improves performance, when in fact only highly motivated staff self-selected into the programme.
Measurement Bias	Happens when data collection tools or processes systematically favour certain outcomes. A faulty scanner that consistently under counts stock levels produces inaccurate inventory data.
Confirmation Bias	When people interpret data in a way that supports their existing beliefs or expectations. A manager who believes a product performs well may ignore negative data and focus only on positive indicators.
Response Bias	Occurs when respondents give inaccurate or incomplete answers, often to appear positive or avoid criticism. Employees answering a staff survey question about job satisfaction more positively because they fear being identified.
Historical Bias	When data reflects past inequalities or patterns, which then influence future decisions. An AI model trained on past hiring data that favoured certain groups may continue those patterns unless corrected.
Algorithmic Bias	Bias created by automated systems or AI if their training data is incomplete, unbalanced or biased. A recommendation engine showing different prices or offers to different customer types based on learned patterns that may be unfair.

3.3.2 Correlation and causation

Understanding the difference between correlation and causation is essential when interpreting data and producing visualisations.

KEY TERM

Correlation: A relationship or association between two variables – when one changes, the other also tends to change.

Causation: When one variable directly influences or produces a change in another.

When looking at data that appears to be correlated it is important to remember that **correlation** does not prove that one variable **causes** the other. For example, ice cream sales and sunburn cases both increase in summer, but ice cream does not cause sunburn – the weather influences both.

Any **causation** must be proved through **evidence**. For example, through statistical analysis it is possible to prove that an increase in advertising spend causes an increase in sales.

The distinction between correlation and causation is important because:

- Misinterpreting correlation as causation can lead to incorrect business decisions.
- Visualisations can make unrelated patterns appear meaningful if not explained correctly.
- Responsible data analysis requires testing whether one factor genuinely causes another.

3.3.3 Ethical issues in data visualisation and data use

Data visualisations and data in general, whilst largely positive for businesses, also have **potentially ethical implications**. Some of which we have already seen. The table below summarises the key issues to be aware of.

Ethical issues related to data visualisations	Ethical issues related to data use
Misleading visuals Visualisations can be designed – intentionally or accidentally – to exaggerate or hide trends. For example: • Distorted scales (eg a y axis that doesn't start at zero) • Manipulated chart types (eg 3D charts that hide differences) • Leaving out relevant data to influence interpretation	**Privacy and consent** Using personal data without proper consent or for purposes not originally stated can breach trust and laws such as GDPR.
Lack of transparency If viewers do not understand where the data came from, how it was collected or what it represents, they may misinterpret the findings. Clear labelling, sources and explanations are essential.	**Fairness** Data should not be used in ways that discriminate against individuals or groups. For example, using biased data to make decisions about lending, hiring or pricing is unethical and potentially unlawful.
Overcomplication Visualisations that are too complex, crowded or technical can confuse audiences, leading to misinterpretation and poor decisions.	**Transparency and accountability** Businesses must be able to explain how data is used, how decisions are made and how algorithms operate.
	Security Poor security puts individuals' information at risk of misuse, fraud or harm. Ethical data use requires strong protection of sensitive information.

Assessment focus point

Presenting data is a rich source of assessment questions. For example, you may be required to interpret visualisations (such as identifying what a visualisation is showing you) and to show an awareness of potential issues with the information you are presented with (such as bias and the difference between correlation and causation). You could also be presented with information and required to identify any possible issues with it (for example being presented with spreadsheet information and being asked to identify causes of errors in it).

Chapter summary

- **Accurate** and **reliable information** is critical to business.
- A **primary source of information** is as close as you can get to the origin of an item of information.
- A **secondary source of information** provides 'second-hand' information, in other words the person or organisation using the information is not the one who originally collected it.
- An organisation may obtain information from **internal** or **external sources**.
- When a business collects data, it must decide whether to **gather information from every member** of the population it is interested in, or whether to **collect data from only a subset** (sample) of that population.
- The main types of **data errors** include systematic errors, random errors, negligent errors, and several other important categories.
- **Data cleansing is** the process of identifying and correcting errors, gaps and inconsistencies within a dataset to ensure that the information a business uses is accurate, complete, reliable and fit for analysis.
- To have value to an organisation, data needs to have meaning. **Data analytics** creates this meaning by assembling, filtering, sorting, highlighting and finally presenting the data in useful forms.
- There are **six principles** to protect data concerning individuals (not businesses). **Lawfulness, fairness and transparency; purpose limitation; data minimisation; accuracy; storage limitation, and integrity and confidentiality**.
- An organisation's **data and information** is a **highly valuable resource**. Not only does it contain important information for business decision making, but it also contains data and other files that are necessary for information and other systems to operate. Any loss or damage to this data will therefore not only impact decisions, but also whether or not day-to-day business operations can continue.
- **Commercially sensitive information** is any data that, if shared without permission, could damage the organisation's competitive position, undermine negotiations or business relationships, reduce profit or market share or lead to legal or regulatory issues.
- When personal or **confidential business data** is accessed, stolen or disclosed without authorisation, the **consequences** on **individuals** and **businesses** can be serious.
- The **sheer volume of data** and **information** that businesses generate creates a risk that recipients of information get caught up in minutiae and **lose sight of the big picture**. The concept of **data visualisation**, is an especially useful way of presenting a wealth of information without it being overwhelming to the user.
- While charts and graphs are important, visualisation alone is not enough. Data needs to be accompanied by a **clear narrative** that explains what the visual is showing and why it matters.
- Modern organisations rely heavily on **digital tools** to collect, analyse, and present data. While these tools can improve efficiency and decision making, they also introduce risks.
- **Biased data** reduces reliability, risks incorrect decision making and can lead to unethical or discriminatory outcomes.
- Understanding the difference between **correlation** and **causation** is essential when interpreting data and producing visualisations.
- Data visualisations and data in general, whilst largely positive for businesses, also have potentially **ethical implications**.

Activity answers

Activity 1: Valid sources of information

Business activity	Information source
Calculating employee pay based on the number of hours worked	Time sheets
Forecasting the country's inflation rate	Government statistics
Costing activities in the production process	Production records
Researching the price of a competitor's products	Company website
Identifying the amount of tax to be paid to HMRC on employee salaries	Payroll system

Activity 2: Providing information

The correct answers are:

	Yes – provide information ✓	No – personal information ✓	No – confidential information ✓
A colleague asks for the email address of a customer so they can contact them about an order they placed	✓		
The partner of a customer asks you for the details of what their partner ordered recently.			✓
The receptionist at head office has requested the names of people due to visit you today.	✓		

Activity 3: Cybersecurity

A Distributed Denial of Service (DDoS) attack is an attempt to disrupt an organisation's online activities by preventing people from accessing the organisation's website. It is conducted using Botnets (large numbers of individual computers which have been taken over without the user knowing). These Botnets are instructed to overwhelm the organisation's website with a wave of internet traffic so that the system is unable to handle it and may cause it to crash.

Test your learning

1 **Which type of error occurs when a value is recorded incorrectly due to a consistent flaw in the measurement process?**

	✓
Random error	
Systematic error	
Transcription error	
Processing error	

2 **Which type of data analytics focuses on understanding why something happened by exploring root causes and relationships within the data?**

	✓
Descriptive analytics	
Predictive analytics	
Diagnostic analytics	
Prescriptive analytics	

3 **Which TWO of the following are recognised principles under data protection laws such as GDPR?**

	✓
Data must be collected for specified, explicit, and legitimate purposes.	
Personal data should be kept indefinitely so future needs can be met.	
Personal data must be accurate and kept up to date.	
Organisations should share personal data with any third party that requests it.	

4 **What is phishing?**

5 **Which of the following is an example of sampling bias in a dataset?**

	✓
Data is collected only from people who respond to an online survey, excluding those without internet access.	
The data analyst accidentally mistypes several values when entering results.	
A sensor records temperatures incorrectly because it is poorly calibrated.	
A model performs poorly because it was trained on high quality images but used on low quality images.	

5 Understanding the importance of sustainability in business

Learning outcomes

5.1 Introduction to sustainability

Learners need to understand:

- Key sustainability concepts:
  - Different forms of capital, the circular economy, economic growth and degrowth
- Global sustainability challenges
- The pillars of sustainability (3 Ps):
  - People, profit, planet
- Challenges to the pillars of sustainability

5.2 Sustainability standards and reporting

Learners need to understand:

- The United Nations Sustainable Development Goals (UN SDGs)
- The actions governments can take to promote sustainability
- The standards applicable to organisations reporting under IFRSs:
  - IFRS S1 General Requirements for Disclosure of Sustainability-related Financial Information
    - Objective to require organisations to disclose sustainability-related risks and opportunities
    - For reporting periods starting after 1 January 2024
    - Includes information on governance processes, strategies for risks and opportunities and performance measures for sustainability targets
  - IFRS S2 Climate-related Disclosures
    - Objective to require organisations to disclose information about their climate-related risks and opportunities
    - For reporting periods starting after 1 January 2024
    - Includes information on governance processes, strategies for risks and opportunities and performance measures for sustainability targets
  - IFRS S2 should be used in conjunction with IFRS S1
- The movement towards prescriptive sustainability guidance.

5.3 Business sustainability

Learners need to understand:

- The actions that businesses can take towards sustainability
- That the actions to promote one pillar of sustainability may impact another pillar
- The benefits of adopting sustainable business practices
- The importance of having a sustainability policy
- The challenges to implementing sustainability policy
- The meaning of:
  - Greenwashing, greenhushing
- The importance of taking responsibility for sustainability:
  - Personal, professional
- How the accountant can contribute to and help manage sustainability.

Learners need to be able to:

- Identify actions to promote sustainability

Assessment context

In the assessment, you may be asked to explain sustainability concepts, interpret the challenges faced by businesses and suggest actions that support environmental, social and economic goals. You should be prepared to refer to sustainability reporting standards such as IFRS S1 and IFRS S2, and to recognise potential issues such as greenwashing.

Qualification context

This chapter builds your understanding of sustainability in a way that supports other units, particularly where long term decision making, governance and reporting are involved. You may already have encountered links between ethics, governance and accountability, but sustainability is explored here in a more structured and detailed way.

Business context

Sustainability has become an essential part of business strategy. Organisations are expected to manage their environmental impact, contribute positively to society and act responsibly over the long term. Understanding sustainability concepts helps you recognise how businesses respond to global challenges and how accounting professionals can support sustainable practices and reporting.

Chapter overview

Understanding the importance of sustainability in business

Introduction to sustainability

- Sustainability
- The circular economy
- Economic growth and degrowth
- Global sustainability challenges
- The pillars of sustainability (3 Ps) and challenges to them

Sustainability standards and reporting

- UN Sustainable Development Goals (UN SDGs)
- Government action
- Organisational reporting under IFRSs
- IFRS S1 General Requirements for Disclosure of Sustainability-related Financial Information
- IFRS S2 Climate-related Disclosures
- Prescriptive sustainability guidance

Business sustainability

- Sustainability responsibilities of business
- Actions businesses can take towards sustainability
- Impacts of sustainability actions
- Sustainability policies and benefits of sustainability
- Greenwashing, greenhushing and other issues
- Accountants and sustainability
- Responsibilities of finance professionals

Introduction

Sustainability has become an increasingly important consideration for organisations operating in a complex and rapidly changing global environment. Businesses are now expected not only to generate profit, but also to act responsibly in relation to their impact on society and the environment. For accounting professionals, this creates a need to understand how sustainability influences business strategy, performance measurement and reporting.

This chapter introduces the key concepts that underpin **sustainability in a business context.** It begins by exploring fundamental ideas such as different forms of capital, the **circular economy,** and the challenges associated with global sustainability issues. The concept of the **three pillars of sustainability—people, profit and planet** – is also examined, alongside the potential conflicts and trade-offs that organisations must manage when balancing these priorities.

The chapter then considers the increasing importance of **sustainability reporting and standards.** You will explore the role of the **United Nations Sustainable Development Goals (SDGs)** and how governments and organisations contribute towards achieving them. In addition, the chapter introduces key reporting frameworks such as **IFRS S1 and IFRS S2**, which require organisations to disclose information about sustainability-related risks, opportunities and performance. This reflects the growing expectation that sustainability is integrated into mainstream financial and strategic reporting.

Finally, the chapter focuses on how sustainability is applied in practice within organisations. It examines the **actions businesses can take** to promote sustainability, the benefits of adopting sustainable practices, and the challenges that may arise when implementing sustainability policies. Concepts such as **greenwashing** and **greenhushing** are also considered, highlighting the importance of transparency and ethical communication. The role of the accountant is emphasised throughout, particularly in supporting decision making, measuring sustainability performance, and ensuring reliable reporting.

By linking sustainability concepts, reporting frameworks and real-world business practices, this chapter demonstrates how sustainability is becoming a central part of organisational effectiveness and accountability. It highlights the important contribution accounting professionals make in supporting organisations to operate responsibly while delivering long-term value for stakeholders.

1 Introduction to sustainability

It is likely that you already know what sustainability is and why it is important. In this section we will consider sustainability from a business perspective and the main challenges that need to be addressed.

1.1 Sustainability

In the modern business world, the concept of **sustainability** is becoming increasingly important.

KEY TERM

> **Sustainability:** According to the **UN's Brundtland Report** (World Commission on Environment and Development, 1987) **sustainability** means that organisations must aim to 'meet the needs of the present without compromising the ability of future generations to meet their own needs'.

There are three aspects to sustainability.

- **Economic sustainability** ensures fair distribution and efficient allocation of global resources. Developed countries consume more per capita than developing countries. Economic growth must be balanced with the needs of the developing world.
- **Social sustainability** involves the responsibility to work towards eradication of human inequality, poverty and social injustice. This responsibility falls particularly heavily on Western firms that employ people in developing countries.

BPP

- **Environmental sustainability** describes the need for organisations to consider how their activities impact the environment and to take steps to minimise that impact and to conserve energy.

The diagram below shows how **economic, social** and **environmental issues** are linked.

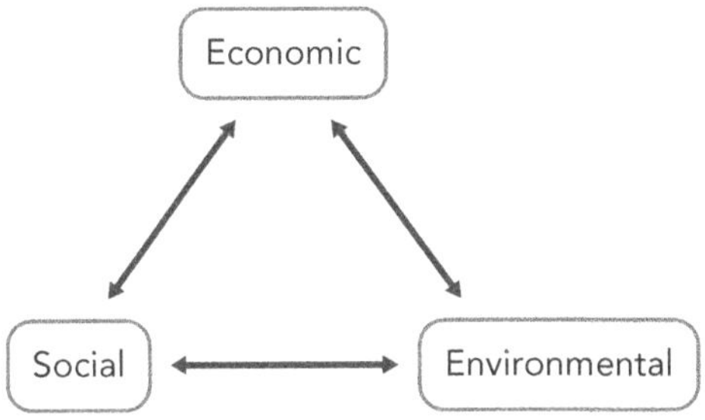

Sustainable development is a core part of any organisation's strategy. It can be seen in policies aimed at reducing waste, using less energy and recycling, as part of the process of decarbonisation. Companies are increasingly engaging in practices such as encouraging flexible working, cycle to work schemes, reducing business travel through the use of technology and sourcing materials from green suppliers. Sustainability is also fostered through research and development, supply chain improvements and innovation.

Some key areas related to sustainability that you need to be aware of are the capitals, circular economy and economic growth and degrowth.

1.1.1 The capitals

The capitals refer to the **resources and relationships** of the organisation. All organisations rely on various forms of capital, not just financial capital, for their success. The capitals are set out in the **Integrated Reporting Framework**, (International <IR> Framework) (IFRS 2016).

KEY TERM

> **Capitals:** The broad categories of resources and relationships that an organisation uses or affects in creating value over time. They represent the different "stocks" of value – financial and non financial – that the organisation draws on as inputs to its business model and that are increased, decreased, or transformed through its activities and outputs. The capitals provide a holistic way of understanding how value is created, preserved, or eroded beyond financial performance alone.

The Framework defines six capitals as follows:

Financial capital

'The pool of funds that is:

- available to an organisation for use in the production of goods or the provision of services
- obtained through financing, such as debt, equity or grants, or generated through operations or investments'

Manufactured capital

'Manufactured physical objects (as distinct from natural physical objects) that are available to an organisation for use in the production of goods or services, including:

- buildings
- equipment
- infrastructure' (eg road, ports, bridges, waste/water treatment plants)

It is 'often created by other organisations, but includes assets manufactured by the reporting organisation for sale or when they are retained for its own use.'

Intellectual capital

'Organisational, knowledge-based intangibles, including:

- intellectual property, such as patents, copyrights, software, rights and licences
- 'organisational capital' such as tacit knowledge, systems, procedures and protocols'

Human capital

'People's competencies, capabilities and experience, and their motivations to innovate, including their:

- alignment with and support for an organisation's governance framework, risk management approach, and ethical values
- ability to understand, develop and implement an organisation's strategy
- loyalties and motivations for improving processes, goods and services, including their ability to lead, manage and collaborate'

Social and relationship capital

'The institutions and relationships within and between communities, groups of stakeholders and other networks, and the ability to share information to enhance individual and collective well-being'.
It includes:

- 'shared norms, and common values and behaviours
- key stakeholder relationships, and the trust and willingness to engage that an organisation has developed and strives to build and protect with external stakeholders
- intangibles associated with the brand and reputation that an organisation has developed
- an organisation's social licence to operate'

Natural capital

'All renewable and non-renewable environmental resources and processes that provide goods or services that support the past, current or future prosperity of an organisation. It includes:

- air, water, land, minerals and forests
- biodiversity and eco-system health'

The capitals are **interrelated** – for example:

- Expenditure on staff training results in an increase in human capital and a decrease in financial capital
- A decision to purchase a new IT system results in an increase in manufactured capital and a decrease in financial capital

Activity 1: Definitions of the capitals

AB is a car manufacturer. Its key assets are:

- Factories
- Plant and machinery
- Warehouses
- Inventory (raw material, work in progress and finished goods)

Required

Under the International <IR> Framework, which category of capital do the above assets relate to?

	✓
Financial capital	
Natural capital	
Manufactured capital	
Social and relationship capital	

1.1.2 The circular economy

The **circular economy is** an economic model designed to keep materials, products and resources in use for as long as possible, reducing waste and minimising the need for new raw materials. Unlike the traditional linear model – often described as "take, make, dispose" – the circular economy aims to eliminate waste through smarter product design, reuse, repair, refurbishment, remanufacturing and high-quality recycling.

The **Ellen MacArthur Foundation** (2026) is one of the key global organisations behind the development, promotion, and mainstream adoption of the circular economy. It describes it as a system built on three core principles: eliminating waste and pollution, circulating products and materials at their highest value, and regenerating nature. This approach directly supports global sustainability goals by reducing reliance on finite resources and cutting the environmental impacts of extraction and processing.

Research also shows that adopting circular practices can significantly reduce greenhouse gas emissions and create economic opportunities, demonstrating how circularity can benefit both the environment and long-term business resilience. By designing out waste and prioritising resource efficiency, businesses can operate more sustainably while also reducing costs, unlocking innovation and increasing competitiveness.

1.1.3 Economic growth and degrowth

Traditional economic growth – the long term increase in the value of goods and services produced – has been central to economic policy since the Industrial Revolution. Growth has historically been associated with **rising living standards**, **technological progress** and **improved health outcomes**. However, modern sustainability research highlights a strong link between **continuous economic growth** and **rising environmental pressures**, including increased carbon emissions, resource depletion and biodiversity loss. This is because economic expansion has relied heavily on energy and resource use, contributing significantly to climate change and pushing ecosystems beyond safe limits.

In contrast, the **concept of degrowth** challenges the assumption that economies must grow indefinitely. Degrowth advocates propose **intentionally reducing production** and **consumption in wealthier countries** to bring human activity back within ecological limits. The idea, which emerged in the 1970s and has gained traction in recent years, emphasises wellbeing, equity and sustainability over GDP expansion. Degrowth therefore focusses on **reducing overconsumption, promoting fairness** in resource distribution, **strengthening local communities** and **prioritising quality of life** rather than material throughput.

While **growth based economies** continue to dominate policy thinking, the debate between **green growth** (growth that reduces environmental impact) and **degrowth** is increasingly influential in sustainability discussions. Both perspectives aim to **address climate change**, but they differ fundamentally in whether long term economic expansion is compatible with ecological limits. Understanding these concepts helps organisations critically assess how their strategies contribute to – or mitigate – environmental risks and supports more informed decision making in the move toward **sustainable business models**.

1.2 Global sustainability challenges

Sustainability challenges today span environmental, economic, and social dimensions, driven by accelerating climate impacts, geopolitical pressures, resource competition, and widening inequalities. There is a growing consensus that without rapid, coordinated global action, many of these challenges are shifting from future risks to present-day realities.

The table below sets out some of the most pressing global sustainability challenges.

Global sustainability challenge	Explanation
Climate change and extreme weather	Climate change remains one of the most severe long-term risks, with impacts already being felt worldwide. Extreme weather events – such as storms, floods, droughts, and heatwaves – are now persistent realities rather than future projections. Without transformative action, global temperatures are likely to continue to rise, driving major economic losses and worsening poverty.
Biodiversity loss and ecosystem collapse	Biodiversity decline, deforestation, and ecosystem collapse are consistently ranked among the top long-term global risks. Current environmental trends point toward potentially catastrophic outcomes unless things change.
Pollution and waste	Pollution – from plastics, chemicals, and particulate matter – continues to worsen. Plastics alone produce significant greenhouse gas emissions throughout their lifecycle, contributing to climate change and harming marine and terrestrial ecosystems. Pollution is a leading cause of premature deaths globally, with many people at risk unless waste and resource systems are fundamentally transformed.

Global sustainability challenge	Explanation
Resource scarcity and geopolitical competition	Competition over vital natural resources – such as rare earth minerals, water, and arable land – is intensifying. Climate-driven changes (for example, Arctic ice melt) are opening new routes and extraction zones, while major powers are investing heavily in resource rich regions to secure materials essential for the energy transition.
Social inequality and economic vulnerability	Environmental crises disproportionately impact vulnerable populations, deepening global inequality. Adopting sustainability policies could lift millions out of undernourishment and extreme poverty, whereas inaction risks severe future economic and social consequences.
Rapid urbanisation and unsustainable development	Ongoing population growth, industrialisation, and urban expansion drive increased resource consumption and environmental degradation. These trends amplify pressures on energy systems, food supplies, water access, and waste management. A shift towards circular economies, sustainable diets, and resilient infrastructure is increasingly important to ensure long term planetary health.

1.3 The pillars of sustainability (3 Ps) and challenges to them

The **three pillars of sustainability** – often referred to as the **triple bottom line** – provide a framework for balancing social equity (**People**), environmental stewardship (**Planet**), and economic viability (**Profit**). This model is widely used to guide organisations toward long term resilience, ethical practice, and sustainable growth. The table below explains each pillar and the challenges that they present.

Pillar	Challenges
People (Social Sustainability) The People pillar focuses on human wellbeing, fair labour practices, community development, diversity, equity, and overall social responsibility. Social sustainability requires companies to consider how their operations affect employees, customers, suppliers, and wider society. Organisations centring people in their strategies often benefit from stronger community relationships, higher employee retention, and improved brand loyalty.	• **Inequality and poor labour standards:** Many global supply chains struggle with unsafe working conditions, wage disparities, and exploitation. • **Lack of stakeholder engagement:** Despite its importance, meaningful engagement with communities and employees is often inconsistent or superficial. • **Social impacts of economic disruption**: Rapid geopolitical and economic shifts increase vulnerability for workers and communities, creating instability.

Pillar	Challenges
Planet (Environmental Sustainability) The Planet pillar stresses responsible use of natural resources, reduction of environmental harm, efficient energy use, and active measures to minimise pollution and carbon emissions. Environmental stewardship has become central to modern sustainability, with organisations expected to adopt green technologies and reduce waste and emissions to remain compliant, competitive, and credible.	• **Climate change and resource depletion:** Businesses must address their environmental footprint amid escalating climate-related risks. • **Pollution and waste management:** Many industries still rely on linear economies, generating excessive waste and increasing emissions. • **Compliance pressure and regulatory expectations:** Firms face growing environmental reporting requirements under various laws, regulations and frameworks. • **Need for technology adoption:** Implementing advanced tools (such as AI) for environmental monitoring is resource intensive, yet increasingly necessary.
Profit (Economic Sustainability) The Profit pillar emphasises maintaining long term financial stability and delivering economic value while avoiding harm to society or the environment. It does not reject profit; rather, it reframes it as part of a balanced system where economic decisions support both social wellbeing and environmental protection. Companies integrating sustainability into financial strategy often gain improved resilience, better investor confidence, and more stable revenue streams.	• **Short termism in business models:** Traditional profit-first thinking can conflict with long term sustainability investments. • **Costs of sustainable transformation:** Transitioning to circular systems, ethical supply chains, or low carbon operations can require substantial upfront capital. • **Economic volatility:** Changing markets, shifting trade routes, and resource constraints create uncertainty for businesses trying to stabilise long-term profitability. • **Measurement and reporting complexity:** Robust sustainability metrics are essential for financial decision making, yet many organisations still lack reliable systems for tracking economic, environmental, and social value creation.

The **pillars of sustainability** represent a holistic framework for guiding organisations toward ethical, resilient, and future focused operations. Yet each pillar faces substantial challenges, from environmental degradation and socioeconomic inequity to pressures created by global instability and regulatory complexity. Addressing these challenges requires **integrated strategies**, **meaningful stakeholder engagement**, and **innovative technologies** that support balance across all three dimensions of sustainable development.

2 Sustainability standards and reporting

In the previous section we looked at what sustainability is from a business perspective and the challenges that it poses us globally. In this section we shall look at one approach to deal with sustainability issues and the increasing requirement that businesses report their progress in meeting the sustainability challenges that are relevant to them.

2.1 UN Sustainable Development Goals (UN SDGs)

The **UN Sustainable Development Goals (SDGs)** are a set of 17 global goals adopted by all UN Member States in 2015 as part of the 2030 Agenda for Sustainable Development. They provide a shared blueprint for ending poverty, protecting the planet, and ensuring peace and prosperity for all by 2030. The goals are integrated, recognising that progress in one area influences outcomes in others, and they require coordinated global action across social, environmental, and economic dimensions.

The **UN Sustainable Development Goals** (SDGs), (UN, 2026)

(a) **No Poverty** – End poverty in all its forms everywhere.

(b) **Zero Hunger** – End hunger, achieve food security, improve nutrition, and promote sustainable agriculture.

(c) **Good Health and Well Being** – Ensure healthy lives and promote wellbeing for all at all ages.

(d) **Quality Education** – Ensure inclusive and equitable quality education and promote lifelong learning opportunities for all.

(e) **Gender Equality** – Achieve gender equality and empower all women and girls.

(f) **Clean Water and Sanitation** – Ensure availability and sustainable management of water and sanitation for all.

(g) **Affordable and Clean Energy** – Ensure access to affordable, reliable, sustainable, and modern energy for all.

(h) **Decent Work and Economic Growth** – Promote sustained, inclusive, and sustainable economic growth, full and productive employment, and decent work for all.

(i) **Industry, Innovation, and Infrastructure** – Build resilient infrastructure, promote inclusive and sustainable industrialisation, and foster innovation.

(j) **Reduced Inequalities** – Reduce inequality within and among countries.

(k) **Sustainable Cities and Communities** – Make cities inclusive, safe, resilient, and sustainable.

(l) **Responsible Consumption and Production** – Ensure sustainable consumption and production patterns.

(m) **Climate Action** – Take urgent action to combat climate change and its impacts.

(n) **Life Below Water** – Conserve and sustainably use oceans, seas, and marine resources.

(o) **Life on Land** – Protect, restore, and promote sustainable use of terrestrial ecosystems; halt biodiversity loss.

(p) **Peace, Justice and Strong Institutions** – Promote peaceful and inclusive societies, provide access to justice, and build effective, accountable institutions.

(q) **Partnerships for the Goals** – Strengthen global partnerships to support implementation of the SDGs.

From a **business perspective**, the UN SDGs provide a **shared global framework** that companies can use to shape strategy, manage risks, and innovate solutions to societal and environmental challenges. In practice, businesses adopt **SDG-aligned policies**, **integrate sustainability into core operations**, and **develop products and services that support goals** such as clean energy, responsible consumption, poverty reduction, and gender equality.

This alignment can **strengthen competitiveness** by building trust with stakeholders, attracting investment, opening new markets, and enhancing long-term resilience. The SDGs also help businesses **identify material impacts** – both positive and negative – and **encourage transparent reporting** and measurable commitments, which remain areas where many firms still need improvement.

The **effectiveness** of the UN SDGs can be viewed as mixed when considered from multiple perspectives. From a **global policy** and **coordination** standpoint, the SDGs have been effective in providing a shared framework and common language for governments, businesses, and civil society to address complex global challenges such as poverty, inequality, climate change, and health. They have **raised awareness**, encouraged **cross sector collaboration**, and **guided national strategies**. However, from an **implementation** perspective, **progress has been uneven** across regions and goals, with **limited resources**, **political instability**, and **weak governance** constraining impact in many countries. Critics also argue that the SDGs are **overly broad and ambitious**, making measurement and accountability difficult. Overall, while the SDGs have been effective as a **vision setting** and **agenda shaping tool**, their success in delivering tangible outcomes depends heavily on national commitment, funding, and translation into concrete local actions.

Real life example

Over 20,000 organisations across 160 countries are currently involved in applying UN SDGS to their activities, including multinational organisations such as Unilever and Microsoft. You can search for participating organisations at https://unglobalcompact.org/what-is-gc/participants.

Assessment focus point

Assessments may require you to identify which UN SDG is being supported by an action by the business in the scenario.

2.2 Government action

Governments play a central role in **advancing sustainability** through **policy, regulation**, **investment** and **public leadership**. Much of what they do filters down from global agreements such as the UN SDGs, but many governments are also proactive in making decisions that keep their country at the forefront of developments in sustainability.

Some key **actions governments** can take to **promote sustainability**:

Promote circular economy practices, such as designing products for durability, repair and recycling, and creating systems that keep materials in circulation for longer. For example, the European Union (EU) does not allow electronics to be designed with a hidden or **built-in limited lifetime** ("planned obsolescence"). Instead, the EU has introduced a set of binding rules that directly target and restrict planned or premature obsolescence, especially in electronic and ICT products.

Governments can **support the transition** to a circular economy by introducing extended producer responsibility (EPR) schemes, funding recycling and repair infrastructure, and providing incentives for low waste business models.

Implementing climate and environmental regulation, such as carbon pricing, emissions standards, pollution controls and incentives for renewable energy adoption. Governments can also invest in sustainable transport, green public procurement, nature restoration projects and education campaigns to promote sustainable consumption.

Supporting fair and inclusive economic systems. Unchecked economic expansion can accelerate environmental damage and push global systems beyond safe planetary boundaries. Policy measures such as promoting local economies, improving resource efficiency, supporting green jobs, and integrating social wellbeing into economic planning can help countries balance prosperity with ecological limits, therefore governments are equipped to lead the transition toward sustainable development and help achieve the SDGs.

2.3 Organisational reporting under IFRSs and prescriptive sustainability guidance

As part of an approach to embed sustainability within business organisations, international accounting standards have been developed in relation to sustainability reporting in financial statements.

The **International Sustainability Standards Board (ISSB)** published its first two standards in June 2023:

- **IFRS S1** General Requirements for Disclosure of Sustainability-related Financial Information
- **IFRS S2** Climate-related Disclosures

The priority of the ISSB is to support the **implementation of these standards** while commencing research projects on biodiversity, ecosystems and ecosystem services, and human capital with a view to publishing further standards on these topics.

IFRS Sustainability Disclosure Standards were endorsed by the International Organisation of Securities Commissions (IOSCO) in July 2023. The IFRS Sustainability Disclosure Standards are **not automatically mandatory** in any country but become so when a **country** or **regulator chooses to adopt them.** They are applicable for accounting periods beginning on or after 1 January 2024 with the first reporting prepared in accordance with IFRS Sustainability Disclosure Standards expected in 2025.The disclosure standards are focussed on the **primary users of financial reports** which are existing and potential investors, lenders and other creditors.

2.4 IFRS S1 General Requirements for Disclosure of Sustainability-related Financial Information

The first standard issued by the ISSB was **IFRS S1 General Requirements for Disclosure of Sustainability-related Financial Information.** This standard sets out the core content for a complete set of sustainability-related financial disclosures to meet the needs of global capital markets.

KEY TERM

> **Value chain:** The full range of interactions, resources and relationships related to a reporting entity's business model and the external environment in which operates. (IFRS S1, Appendix A)

2.4.1 Scope and objective of IFRS S1

IFRS S1 states that the **objective of the standard** is to 'require an entity to disclose information about its sustainability-related risks and opportunities that is useful to primary users of general purpose financial reports in making decisions relating to providing resources to the entity'. (IFRS S1, para 1)

Under IFRS S1, the primary users of general purpose financial reports are existing and potential investors, lenders and other creditors. Other stakeholders such as customers and employees are not considered to be primary users.

Information about sustainability-related risks and opportunities is useful to the primary users because the cash-generating capability of an entity comes from the necessary interactions between its stakeholders, society, the economy and the natural environment through the entities value chain. (IFRS S1, para 2, 3)

The **value chain** includes the product/services of the entity, human resources, marketing and distribution, procurement, sales and delivery, financing, legal etc.

An **entity preparing sustainability-related financial disclosure**s in accordance with IFRS Sustainability Disclosure Standards must apply IFRS S1 and any other relevant standard. Although IFRS Sustainability Disclosure Standards are designed to work alongside IFRS Accounting Standards, entities can use other generally accepted financial reporting standards.

2.4.2 Core content and general requirements of IFRS S1

IFRS S1 requires a company to prepare disclosures about how it manages its sustainability related risks and opportunities (SROs) under four headings: governance, strategy, risk management and metrics and targets (IFRS S1, para 25).

Governance	Strategy
The governance process, controls and procedures used to monitor and manage SROs, eg: • Who has responsibility for SROs overall, and in practice? • Who oversees the setting of targets and metrics?	The approach used to manage SROs, including information that enables investors to understand the current and anticipated financial effects of SROs on the company's financial position, performance and cashflows over the short, medium and long term, eg: • The effects of SROs on the business and value chain • The resilience of the entity to SROs

Risk Management	Metrics and Targets
The process to identify, evaluate, prioritise and monitor SROs, eg: • How risks are assessed and prioritised • How SROs are integrated into the overall risk management of the entity	Performance in relation to SROs including progress towards any targets required by law or regulation eg: • The metrics used and any target • The base period from which progress is measured

IFRS S1 also requires entities to consider the **most recent requirements of other sustainability-related standard setting bodies** as well as the SROs identified by other entities that operating in the same industry or geographic region.

The **sustainability-related reporting** should be made at the same time, and for the same reporting period, as the related financial statements. Comparative information should be disclosed for numerical and narrative information.

Activity 2: IFRS S1

Which TWO of the following statements about IFRS S1 are correct?

	✓
Entities can only apply IFRS S1 if they already apply IFRS Accounting Standards	
Entities should disclose information about the approach taken to manage sustainability-related risks and opportunities	
The objective of IFRS S1 is to provide sustainability-related financial information for all stakeholders	
IFRS S1 requires an entity to consider the requirements of other sustainability-related standard setters	

2.5 IFRS S2 Climate-related Disclosures

IFRS S2 Climate-related disclosures is the first subject-specific ISSB Standard. It requires disclosure of the climate-related risks and opportunities that could reasonably be expected to affect the entity's financial prospects.

IFRS S2 applies to:

(a) Climate-related risks to which the entity is exposed, which are:

- Climate-related physical risks
- Climate-related transition risks

(b) Climate-related opportunities available to the entity

(IFRS S2, para 3)

These terms can be defined as follows:

KEY TERM

Climate-related physical risks : Risks arising from climate-related events or changes e.g. hurricanes or rising sea temperatures

Acute climate-related physical risks : Event-drive climate-related risks relating to weather-related events such as storms, floods, drought or heatwaves.

Chronic climate-related physical risks : Longer-term shifts in climatic patterns including changes in precipitation and temperature which have an impact on the environment eg reduced water availability, biodiversity loss

Climate-related transition risks : Policy, legal, technological, market and reputational risks that arise from the transition to a lower-carbon economy

Climate-related opportunities : The potential positive effects arising from climate change for an entity.

IFRS S2 Appendix A

Many companies and economic sectors face risks from both climate change and from the transition to a lower-carbon economy. There has been an increase in the frequency and severity of climate-related physical risks, as a result of global temperature increases. Both acute and chronic physical risks can have financial implications for an entity on all aspects of the value chain e.g. increase supplier prices, property damage, employee health and safety.

Climate-related transition risks arise from different influences such as:

- Policy and legal risks eg carbon emission legislation
- Technology risk eg unsuccessful investment in new technology
- Market risk eg change in demand
- Reputation risk eg loss of customers

2.5.1 Core content and metrics IFRS S2

The core content of IFRS S2 follows the same format as set out in S1: governance, strategy, risk management and metrics and targets but with a focus on climate-related risks and opportunities.

IFRS S1 introduced the idea of using **metrics and targets** to allows the primary users to measure the performance of the entity. IFRS S2 requires all entities to disclose metrics about greenhouse gas (GHG) emissions, as well as a number of other metrics.

The standard also requires the **disclosure of any climate-related targets** set to monitor progress towards achieving climate-related strategic goals, and any targets required by law or regulation. This includes information such as the metric used to measure progress, the objective of the target, the period to which it applies, the base period and any milestones or interim targets.

Activity 3: IFRS S2

Annual increases in the number of global wildfires as a result of rising temperatures leading to an increase in global timber prices is an example of:

	✓
A climate-related opportunity for a timber producer located in an area affected by wildfires	
A chronic climate-related physical risk for a timber producer located in an area affected by wildfires	
A climate-related transition risk for a timber producer located in an area affected by wildfires	
An acute climate-related physical risk for a timber producer located in an area affected by wildfires	

2.6 The movement towards prescriptive sustainability guidance

As can be seen from the development of IFRS S1 and S2, sustainability reporting has shifted from a voluntary, flexible activity towards a far more prescriptive and standardised approach.

Prescriptive sustainability guidance refers to reporting requirements that set out specific, detailed, and mandatory disclosures that organisations must provide, in contrast to the previously fragmented landscape of voluntary frameworks. Standards such as the IFRS Sustainability Disclosure Standards (S1 and S2) have emerged to create a high quality global baseline of investor focused sustainability information, designed to ensure consistency, comparability and decision usefulness across markets.

The move toward prescriptive guidance is driven by several powerful trends.

- **Investors and capital markets** require **reliable**, **comparable information**, particularly on climate and other sustainability related risks that can materially affect business performance; inconsistent voluntary reporting has created gaps, complexity, and limited comparability.
- **Regulators** worldwide are increasingly adopting or mandating sustainability standards to **enhance transparency** and a**ccountability**.
- As **sustainability issues** become more financially and **strategically significant**, prescriptive standards help ensure that all companies report in a clear, comparable, and trustworthy way – strengthening market confidence and supporting the global transition to a more sustainable economy.

3 Business sustainability

Having previously seen what sustainability is and the move towards more and more reporting of sustainability in financial statements, in this final section we shall now consider the **responsibilities** that businesses and individuals have in relation to sustainability.

3.1 Sustainability responsibilities of business

At the start of the chapter we saw that there are **three aspects to sustainability** (economic, social and environmental). Responsibilities that business has for sustainability can also be grouped into these areas.

Economic responsibilities include supporting the organisation or clients to be profitable, supporting local businesses when choosing suppliers and paying them on time and looking for ways to improve the efficiency of the organisation's finance operations.

Social responsibilities may include supporting policies on corporate governance and consulting the local community when making decisions on investing in or relocating operations.

Environmental responsibilities are usually focused on using less energy (net-zero or zero-carbon activities), carefully using natural resources and creating less pollution.

It is important to realise that there is very often a **trade-off** between acting in a **sustainable way** and **making profit**. This is because sustainable options are often more expensive than non-sustainable ones and therefore a business must choose whether to reduce its profitability to act in a sustainable manner.

3.2 Sustainability actions, practices and policies

With the economic, social and environmental responsibilities in mind, what can businesses do in a practical sense to promote sustainability?

3.2.1 Actions businesses can take towards sustainability

The following table sets out some key actions businesses can take.

Action	Explanation
Switch to renewable energy For example, transitioning from fossil fuels to renewable sources such as solar, wind, or hydro power.	Renewable energy reduces greenhouse gas emissions, helping limit global warming and cutting long term operational costs.
Improve energy efficiency For example, implementing energy efficient technologies (LED lighting and smart systems) and reducing unnecessary energy use.	Lower energy consumption reduces carbon emissions and reduces business overheads.

Action	Explanation
Optimise the supply chain For example, auditing suppliers, choosing low carbon partners, reducing transport emissions, and improving logistics efficiency.	Supply chains represent major sources of emissions, so optimising them significantly cuts environmental impact and supports responsible sourcing.
Reduce waste and increase recycling Minimising packaging, reducing printing, recycling materials, and adopting circular economy approaches.	Less waste reduces pollution, lowers landfill impact, and encourages more efficient resource use.
Develop sustainable products and services Designing products with lower environmental impact, using eco-friendly materials, or creating services that reduce resource consumption.	Supporting sustainable consumption and production helps conserve natural resources and appeal to eco conscious consumers.
Engage employees and stakeholders Training employees on sustainability, gathering stakeholder input, and encouraging participation in sustainability initiatives.	Engagement builds accountability, strengthens company culture, and ensures long term commitment to environmental and social goals.
Adopt circular economy principles Reusing materials, designing for longevity, and reducing dependence on virgin resources.	Circular systems minimise waste, reduce environmental damage, and improve resource efficiency.
Partner with local communities Supporting local initiatives, collaborating with community groups, and contributing to local environmental or social projects.	Supporting local initiatives, collaborating with community groups, and contributing to local environmental or social projects.
Measure and report metrics such as carbon emissions Develop systems to capture and report on sustainability metrics.	Measurement identifies, for example, major emission sources, enabling targeted reduction strategies and improving transparency.

Assessment focus point

Be prepared to identify appropriate actions that a business can take to promote sustainability in a given situation.

3.2.2 Impacts of sustainability actions

As we have seen, sustainability has **three interconnected pillars** (environmental, social and economic). Because these pillars are closely linked, actions designed to improve performance in one area can create positive or negative consequences in another. This happens because real-world systems – such as supply chains, energy use, labour markets and natural resources – are interconnected.

Understanding these trade-offs helps organisations design **balanced sustainability strategies**. For example:

- A **company switches to renewable energy to reduce its carbon footprint** (environmental action affecting the economic pillar). While environmentally beneficial, the transition may require high upfront investment, affecting short term profitability and cashflow.
- A **business reduces water usage by automating part of its production process** (environmental action affecting the social pillar). Automation may improve sustainability but could reduce the number of manual jobs, negatively affecting local employment.

- A **company improves working conditions by increasing indoor ventilation and lighting** (social action affecting the environmental pillar). This raises energy consumption, potentially increasing the organisation's carbon emissions unless renewable energy is used.
- A **business expands production to meet growing consumer demand** (economic action affecting the environmental pillar). Greater production may require more raw materials and energy, raising emissions and waste generation.
- A **firm increases wages to ensure fair pay** (social action affecting the economic pillar). This improves social wellbeing but raises operating costs, affecting profit margins unless offset by productivity gains.

3.2.3 Sustainability policies and benefits of sustainability

A **sustainability policy** is an organisation's formal commitment to operating in a way that minimises negative environmental impacts, supports social wellbeing and ensures long term economic resilience. It sets out the organisation's **sustainability goals,** the **principles it** follows, and the **practical steps** it intends to take. A sustainability policy provides a **clear framework for** decision making, helping employees understand expectations around issues such as resource use, waste reduction, ethical behaviour, community impact and long term environmental stewardship. It acts as a **guiding document** that shapes how the organisation plans, procures, manages risks and reports on its sustainability performance.

Adopting sustainable practices offers **several key benefits**. For example:

- **Environmentally,** organisations can reduce their carbon footprint, cut waste and improve resource efficiency.
- **Socially,** sustainability can enhance workplace wellbeing, strengthen community relationships and support ethical supply chains.
- **Economically**, sustainable practices often lead to cost savings through efficiency improvements, while also enhancing brand reputation and building resilience as customer and investor expectations evolve.
- Many organisations also find that strong sustainability performance improves their **ability to attract talent,** access new markets and prepare for future regulation.

Having a **sustainability policy** is important because it **provides structure, consistency** and **accountability**. Without a policy, sustainability efforts may be fragmented, inconsistent or dependent on individual departments rather than embedded across the organisation.

A policy **signals to stakeholders** – employees, customers, regulators and investors – that the organisation takes sustainability seriously. It supports transparency by clarifying what the organisation intends to achieve and how it will measure progress. It also helps ensure long term commitment, remaining in place even as personnel or business priorities change.

However, implementing a sustainability policy can be challenging.

- Organisations may face **financial constraints** when investing in new technologies or processes, especially where environmental improvements require upfront capital.
- There may also be **cultural resistance** if employees or suppliers are unfamiliar with sustainable practices or see them as adding complexity.
- In some cases, organisations struggle with **limited data,** making it difficult to measure impacts or track progress accurately.
- **Balancing sustainability goals** with **operational demands** – such as maintaining profitability or meeting tight deadlines – can also create tensions.

Despite these challenges, a **well-designed policy** helps organisations move forward with clarity and purpose, ensuring sustainability becomes an integral part of everyday operations rather than an optional extra.

Activity 4: Identifying issues and aspects

Identify which sustainability initiatives have an environmental aspect:

	✓
Ensuring well-fitted windows and doors to prevent heat loss	
Selecting suppliers who operate fair employment practices	
Encouraging a staff charity committee to help raise funds for local community projects	
Programming movement sensors to turn off unnecessary lighting	
Having monthly team meetings by video conference, rather than requiring staff to travel to one location	

3.2.4 Greenwashing, greenhushing and other issues

Businesses today face a growing range of **reputational** and **operational risks** linked to how they **communicate** and **manage their sustainability performance**. Several forms of misleading or selective sustainability communication have emerged, each creating different challenges for organisations.

- **Greenwashing** (including unintentional greenwashing) occurs when a business overstates or exaggerates its environmental commitments or achievements. Sometimes this is intentional, but it can also happen unintentionally when companies set ambitious sustainability goals that they lack the capability or resources to achieve. For example, it might occur where an organisation is under market pressure to pledge Net Zero. Greenwashing can damage trust, attract regulatory scrutiny and expose organisations to legal or financial penalties if claims prove inaccurate.
- **Greenhushing** is the practice in which a company intentionally under-communicates or stays silent about its genuine sustainability achievements, even when those achievements are real and measurable. It often happens because companies fear public scrutiny, activist criticism, or accusations of greenwashing, leading them to avoid drawing attention to their environmental progress. As a result, meaningful sustainability efforts remain hidden, reducing transparency and limiting the ability of investors, consumers, and stakeholders to understand a company's true impact.
- **Greenlighting** is when a business highlights a small, specific or minor 'green' initiative to draw attention away from wider, more damaging environmental impacts. By selectively promoting a single positive action, companies risk misleading stakeholders about their overall performance. This can harm credibility when inconsistencies become visible.
- **Greencrowding** refers to companies joining large sustainability groups or industry initiatives as a way to hide within the crowd. By being part of a broad coalition, individual companies may assume reduced scrutiny and accountability, sometimes while lobbying against stricter environmental policies. This behaviour weakens genuine collective progress and poses reputational risks when uncovered.
- **Bluewashing** involves overstating ethical or socially responsible actions – such as labour practices, diversity or human rights commitments – to appear more ethical than the business actually is. This form of 'social washing' undermines stakeholder trust and can backfire if working conditions or ethical standards fail to match public claims.
- **Brownspinning** is when a business attempts to reframe environmentally harmful activities in a positive way. This often involves presenting a slow or minimal transition away from fossil fuels as meaningful progress. Brownspinning can mislead investors and consumers and may result in accusations of dishonesty once the true impact of operations is reassessed.
- **Greenflation** refers to rising costs associated with sustainable materials or production methods. While some cost increases are legitimate due to supply constraints or new

technologies, greenflation can also be used as an excuse for broader price hikes. Customers, regulators and investors may become sceptical of sustainability related pricing if it appears opportunistic or unjustified.

Together, these issues illustrate the importance of **transparent, evidence based sustainability communication**. Companies that engage in misleading practices face significant risks to reputation, market trust, regulatory compliance and long term value creation.

> **Assessment focus point**
>
> Assessments may test your ability to identify issues such as greenwashing and greenhushing from information given to you.

3.3 Accountants and sustainability

Taking **responsibility for sustainability is** essential because meaningful progress depends not only on organisational policies but also on the actions and decisions made by individuals.

On a **personal level**, responsibility means **being aware of how everyday behaviours** – such as energy use, waste generation, purchasing choices and travel – affect the environment and society. Small, consistent actions by individuals can collectively reduce environmental impact, support ethical supply chains and create demand for more sustainable products and services. Personal responsibility also helps shape a culture where **sustainability** becomes a **normal part of daily decision making** rather than an optional extra.

At a **professional level**, responsibility for sustainability means **ensuring that the decisions made within a role or department support long term environmental, social and economic wellbeing**. This applies to everyone in an organisation, not just senior leaders. Professionals may influence sustainability through procurement choices, project planning, budgeting, risk management, product design or how they work with suppliers and customers. When employees take responsibility for considering sustainability in their roles, organisations become more resilient, compliant and aligned with stakeholder expectations. It also helps prevent issues such as greenwashing or poor ethical practices by encouraging transparency, accountability and integrity in business operations.

3.3.1 Responsibilities of finance professionals

As part of the business world, **finance professionals have** a duty to consider the economic, social and environmental aspects of their work in order to support sustainability.

There are six main responsibilities of finance professionals in regard to upholding the principles of sustainability.

Responsibilities of finance professionals	Explanation
Creating and promoting a sustainability culture	Finance professionals should help senior management create and promote a sustainable culture within their organisation. Primarily it means supporting sustainable policies as they are introduced, but it also means discouraging wasteful or environmentally unfriendly behaviour if they are aware of it.
Championing the aims of sustainability	The aims of sustainability, as identified by the UN's Brundtland Report, should be promoted and followed. However, the finance professional should remain objective at all times. This means that the aims should not be followed blindly, but instead be followed within the context of the organisation's culture and its own policies on sustainability.

Responsibilities of finance professionals	Explanation
Evaluating and quantifying reputational and other ethical risks	Finance professionals have well-developed analysis and evaluation skills. This means they are among the best placed within an organisation to deal with reputational and other ethical risks, including risks to the environment.
Taking social, environmental and economic factors into account when making decisions	Social, environmental and economic factors are together known as the 'triple bottom line'. Many organisations demonstrate their commitment to CSR by including in their financial reports organisational performance information based on these factors. Financial professionals have a responsibility to take these factors into account when making decisions so that, when organisational position and performance is measured, the business can clearly demonstrate its commitment to CSR.
Promoting sustainable practices	As well as promoting policies in relation to ethical and illegal practices, finance professionals should support sustainability practices developed by the organisation. Such practices may be in relation to, for example, products and services, customers, employees, the workplace, supply chain and business functions and processes.
Raising awareness of social responsibility	As mentioned earlier, finance professionals should consider the sustainability impacts of their decisions and actions. By doing so, they will help raise awareness of sustainability within the organisation as colleagues, who may be in different departments, see them taking a lead in this area.

Assessment focus point

Be prepared to recommend actions that finance professionals can support to promote sustainability.

Activity 5: Sustainability

Think of some examples of sustainability issues in the place that you work or study.

Chapter summary

- According to the **UN's Brundtland Report** (World Commission on Environment and Development, 1987) **sustainability** means that organisations must aim to 'meet the needs of the present without compromising the ability of future generations to meet their own needs'.
- The **six capitals** are the broad categories of resources and relationships that an organisation uses or affects in creating value over time.
- The **circular economy is** an economic model designed to keep materials, products and resources in use for as long as possible, reducing waste and minimising the need for new raw materials.
- The **concept of degrowth** challenges the assumption that economies must grow indefinitely.
- **Sustainability challenges** today span environmental, economic, and social dimensions, driven by accelerating climate impacts, geopolitical pressures, resource competition, and widening inequalities.
- The **three pillars of sustainability** – often referred to as the **triple bottom line** – provide a framework for balancing social equity (**People**), environmental stewardship (**Planet**), and economic viability (**Profit**).
- The **UN Sustainable Development Goals (SDGs)** are a set of 17 global goals adopted by all UN Member States in 2015 as part of the 2030 Agenda for Sustainable Development. They provide a shared blueprint for ending poverty, protecting the planet, and ensuring peace and prosperity for all by 2030.
- The **International Sustainability Standards Board (**ISSB) published its first two standards in June 2023. They are **IFRS S1** General Requirements for Disclosure of Sustainability-related Financial Information and **IFRS S2** Climate-related Disclosures.
- For businesses, it is important to realise that there is very often a **trade-off** between acting in a **sustainable way** and **making profit**. This is because sustainable options are often more expensive than non-sustainable ones and therefore a business must choose whether to reduce its profitability to act in a sustainable manner.
- Understanding these trade-offs helps organisations design **balanced sustainability strategies**.
- **Greenwashing** occurs when a business overstates or exaggerates its environmental commitments or achievements.
- **Greenhushing** is the practice in which a company intentionally under-communicates or stays silent about its genuine sustainability achievements, even when those achievements are real and measurable.
- As part of the business world, **finance professionals have** a duty to consider the economic, social and environmental aspects of their work in order to support sustainability.

Activity answers

Activity 1: Definitions of the capitals

The correct answer is:

	✓
Financial capital	
Natural capital	
Manufactured capital	✓
Social and relationship capital	

Response option	Explanation
Financial capital	Financial capital relates to the entity's funds rather than its physical assets.
Natural capital	Natural capital relates to environmental resources and processes rather than manufactured assets.
Manufactured capital	All the assets listed are manufactured physical objects (rather than natural physical objects) that are available for AB to use in the production of goods (cars). Manufactured capital includes assets manufactured for sale (inventory).
Social and relationship capital	This refers to institutions and relationships rather than physical assets.

Activity 2: IFRS S1

The correct answers are:

	✓
Entities can only apply IFRS S1 if they already apply IFRS Accounting Standards	
Entities should disclose information about the approach taken to manage sustainability-related risks and opportunities	✓
The objective of IFRS S1 is to provide sustainability-related financial information for all stakeholders	
IFRS S1 requires an entity to consider the requirements of other sustainability-related standard setters	✓

Response options	Explanation
Entities can only apply IFRS S1 if they already apply IFRS Accounting Standards	IFRS Sustainability Disclosure Standards can be followed by any entity. The entity does not need to also apply IFRS Accounting Standards.

Response options	Explanation
Entities should disclose information about the approach taken to manage sustainability-related risks and opportunities	One of the core areas of content of IFRS S1 is Strategy which is the approach taken by the entity to manage SROs.
The objective of IFRS S1 is to provide sustainability-related financial information for all stakeholders	The IFRS Sustainability Disclosure Standards are focussed on the primary users of general purpose financial information which is current and potential investors, lenders and other creditors.
IFRS S1 requires an entity to consider the requirements of other sustainability-related standard setters	IFRS S1 does require an entity to consider the requirements of other sustainability-related standard setters when determining the most appropriate disclosures.

Activity 3: IFRS S2

The correct answer is:

	✓
A climate-related opportunity for a timber producer located in an area affected by wildfires	
A chronic climate-related physical risk for a timber producer located in an area affected by wildfires	✓
A climate-related transition risk for a timber producer located in an area affected by wildfires	
An acute climate-related physical risk for a timber producer located in an area affected by wildfires	

Response option	Explanation
Climate-related opportunities	The increase in timber prices is a risk rather than an opportunity
Chronic climate-related physical risks	Rising temperatures are an example of a chronic climate-related issue, which in this case has led to wildfires which affect the area where the business is based. Therefore, it represents a risk to the business.
Climate-related transition risks	Climate-related transition risks arise from the transition to a lower-carbon economy, which is not the case here.
Acute climate-related physical risks	Acute climate-related risks are weather-related events such as storms, floods, drought or heatwaves. The annual increase in wildfires is a chronic change, rather than an acute one-off event.

Activity 4: Identifying issues and aspects

The correct answers are:

	✓
Ensuring well-fitted windows and doors to prevent heat loss	✓
Selecting suppliers who operate fair employment practices	
Encouraging a staff charity committee to help raise funds for local community projects	
Programming movement sensors to turn off unnecessary lighting	✓
Having monthly team meetings by video conference, rather than requiring staff to travel to one location	✓

- Environmental – as it reduces fuel consumption (also economic as it saves fuel cost)
- Environmental – as in (a), it also has an economic aspect
- Environmental – less travel is needed, leading to less pollution (also economic aspect as less travel may mean less cost)

Note. 2. Social - as it supports people; 3. Social - as it benefits the local community

Activity 5: Sustainability

Your answer will depend on the nature of your job and the type of organisation that you work for. Good answers would include issues relating to economic factors, social factors and the environment.

Test your learning

1 **Which one of the following statements best describes sustainability?**

	✓
Policies aimed at improving efficiency including reducing waste, using less energy and recycling	
A long-term programme involving a series of sustainable development practices aimed at improving organisational efficiency, stakeholder support and market edge	
A core part of an organisation's corporate social responsibility comprising efficiency, stakeholder support and market edge	

2 **What are the six capitals of the Integrated Reporting Framework?**

3 **Which THREE of the following are part of the scope of IFRS S2?**

	✓
Climate-related topical risks	
Adverse climate-related opportunities	
Climate-related transition risks	
Chronic climate-related physical risks	
Acute climate-related changes	
Climate-related opportunities	

4 **Which of the following statements about IFRS Sustainability Disclosure Standards is true?**

	✓
IFRS Sustainability Disclosure Standards are issued by the IFRS Accounting Standards Board	
IFRS Sustainability Disclosure Standard have replaced the Integrated Reporting Framework	
There are currently 19 IFRS Sustainability Disclosure Standards in issue	
The sustainability disclosures required by the IFRS Sustainability Disclosure Standards are targeted at the primary users of general purpose financial reporting	

5 **Which of the following best describes the difference between greenwashing and greenhushing?**

	✓
Greenwashing is when a company under communicates its sustainability efforts, while greenhushing is when it exaggerates them to appear more ecofriendly.	
Greenwashing is the act of deceptively overstating sustainability claims, whereas greenhushing is intentional silence or under communication about genuine sustainability actions.	
Greenwashing and greenhushing both refer to misleading claims about sustainability, but greenhushing involves providing too much technical detail.	
Greenwashing is always accidental, while greenhushing is always deliberate.	

Test your learning answers

Chapter 1

1 | Vision | is/are the organisation's view of where it sees itself going in the long term

An organisation's mission is its basic purpose and what it is trying to achieve. Strategy and objectives are steps to follow to achieve the vision and mission.

2 The correct answer is:

	✓
Customer	
Internal business	
Innovation and learning	✓
Financial	

Customer measures often focus on quality, delivery time, performance and service.

Internal business measures will focus on processes that are important to meeting customer expectations such as quality, time and cost.

Innovation and learning measures are concerned with improving key internal processes and creating value for customers.

Financial measures – successful strategies should create value for shareholders. Measures will normally cover survival (cash flow), success (sales or profit) and prosperity (shareholder value).

3 The correct answer is:

	✓
Employment levels	
The volume of goods businesses are willing to supply	✓
Interest rates charged by banks	
Level of aggregate demand	

Supply of goods is a micro-economic factor.

4 Governments may provide financial incentives for investment in certain areas. Such incentives are known as | grants | .

Government financial incentives for investments are known as grants.

5 The correct answers are:

	✓
Strengths	✓
Weaknesses	✓
Opportunities	
Threats	

Strengths and weaknesses are internal to an organisation. Opportunities and threats are part of the wider business environment.

Chapter 2

1 The correct answer is:

Task	Category
Preparing a bank reconciliation by the end of next week	Not urgent but important
Deleting old or actioned emails	Not urgent or important
Preparing a document needed for a directors meeting in the morning	Urgent and important
Buying tea and coffee for the staff break room when they have run out	Urgent but not important

2 The correct answer is:

	✓
Sharing financial reports only when asked to avoid overwhelming colleagues	
Presenting complex financial information in clear, accessible language tailored to the audience	✓
Using as much technical terminology as possible to sound professional	
Sending emails instead of speaking to colleagues to save time	

Finance professionals must adapt their communication to suit non-financial audiences, ensuring information is clear, relevant and easy to understand.

Sharing financial reports only when asked to avoid overwhelming colleagues is incorrect because proactive communication is often essential.

Using as much technical terminology as possible to sound professional is incorrect because excessive technical language can confuse non-financial colleagues.

Sending emails instead of speaking to colleagues to save time is incorrect because choosing the right communication method – not the quickest – is key to effectiveness.

3 The correct answer is:

	✓
Completing all analysis personally to ensure accuracy, even when team members have capacity.	
Passing on tasks you find uninteresting without offering support or context.	
Assigning part of a financial review to a junior colleague, providing clear guidance and checking progress at agreed points.	✓
Delegating critical decisions to colleagues without confirming whether they have the necessary skills.	

Effective delegation involves giving someone a clear task, providing context and expectations, and offering appropriate support while still maintaining accountability. For finance professionals, this builds team capability, reduces bottlenecks, and strengthens overall accuracy and efficiency.

Doing everything yourself limits team development, slows down workflows, and increases the risk of burnout. Delegation is important for building a resilient finance function.

Delegating tasks simply to avoid them – without guidance – leads to confusion, errors, and reduced team morale. Effective delegation is purposeful and supportive.

Delegating decisions without ensuring someone has the right skills or authority can create risk, particularly in finance. Proper delegation requires matching tasks to the person's capability and providing appropriate oversight.

4 The correct answer is:

	✓
Having a workforce made up of individuals with different backgrounds, perspectives, and experiences	✓
Employing people only from groups that are under represented	
Ensuring every employee receives identical support regardless of their needs	
Allowing managers to choose team members based solely on personal preference	

A workforce made up of individuals with different backgrounds, perspectives, and experiences is the correct description of diversity because it focuses on variety within the workforce and recognises that different viewpoints strengthen an organisation.

Employing people only from under represented groups is incorrect because diversity is about inclusion of all groups, not prioritising one set over another.

Ensuring every employee receives identical support ignores that people may require different types of support.

Allowing managers to choose team members based solely on personal preference is not diversity; it risks bias and reduces the range of perspectives in the organisation.

5 The correct answer is:

	✓
To ensure all employees receive the same training, regardless of their need	
To create fair access, remove barriers, and support a workplace where different people can contribute fully	✓
To prioritise diversity targets over employee performance	
To ensure only HR is responsible for managing workplace behaviour	

Creating fair access, removing barriers, and supporting a workplace where different people can contribute fully is the correct description because EDI policies are designed to promote fairness, inclusion, and equal opportunity for all employees.

Ensuring all employees receive the same training regardless of need is incorrect because EDI policies recognise that different people may require different forms of support.

Prioritising diversity targets over performance is incorrect because EDI policies are not about lowering standards; they aim to create a fair environment in which everyone can perform at their best.

Ensuring only HR is responsible for workplace behaviour is also incorrect, as EDI is a shared responsibility across the whole organisation, not just a single department.

Chapter 3

1 The correct answer is:

	✓
True	
False	✓

Group values are very important, eg in families and friendship groups (which is where we get our ideas from), national cultures and organisations (which establish ethical norms and expectations by which we have to operate).

2 The correct answer is:

	✓
Say that you will get back to him when you have looked up the answer.	
Give him the contact details of a friend in your firm who knows all about accounting standards.	
Clarify the limits of your expertise with the client.	✓

This is an issue of technical competence and due care. You should clarify the limits of your expertise with the client, and **then** seek information or guidance from the relevant source.

3 The correct answer is:

	✓
True	✓
False	

Straightforwardness and honesty are related to the fundamental principle of integrity.

4 The correct answer is:

	✓
The worker is entitled to keep his job	
The employer is liable to a fine	
The worker will be deemed automatically unfairly dismissed if they lose their job	✓
The employer must make a written apology to the worker	

Whether the employee is entitled to keep their job is at the discretion of the court. With respect to the other options, the Act affords protection to the worker rather than imposing sanctions on the employer.

5 The correct answer is:

	✓
Only report suspicious activity if the client gives permission.	
Wait until full evidence of criminal activity is confirmed before taking any action.	
Share suspicions with colleagues informally before deciding whether to report.	
Submit an internal report to the firm's nominated officer whenever there is knowledge or suspicion of money laundering.	✓

Submitting an internal report to the firm's nominated officer when there is knowledge or suspicion of money laundering reflects the accountant's core obligation under UK money laundering rules. This ensures suspicions are assessed properly and, if necessary, escalated to the authorities through a Suspicious Activity Report (SAR). It helps the accountant meet legal duties and protects the firm from risk.

Permission from the client should never be sought because reporting suspicions must be done confidentially and independently of the client. Waiting for full evidence is also inappropriate because the law requires action based on suspicion, not proof. Discussing suspicions informally with colleagues is risky and may amount to unlawful 'tipping off', which is prohibited under the legislation.

Chapter 4

1 The correct answer is:

	✓
Random error	
Systematic error	✓
Transcription error	
Processing error	

Systematic errors occur when something is consistently wrong in the measurement process – such as a mis calibrated instrument or a biased method.

Random errors happen unpredictably and are caused by small, uncontrollable variations (eg, slight differences in repeated measurements). They do not follow a pattern and are not caused by a consistent flaw. Transcription errors happen when data is copied incorrectly (eg, typing 56 instead of 65). This is a human copying mistake, not a consistent measurement flaw. Processing errors occur when data is incorrectly handled by software or formulas (eg, a wrong calculation in a spreadsheet). Again, this is not related to a consistent measurement flaw.

2 The correct answer is:

	✓
Descriptive analytics	
Predictive analytics	
Diagnostic analytics	✓
Prescriptive analytics	

Diagnostic analytics answers "Why did it happen?", using techniques like data drilling, correlations, and root cause analysis.

Descriptive analytics answers the question "What happened?" by summarising historical data using charts, totals, averages, etc.

It does not investigate causes or deeper reasons behind the results. Predictive analytics answers "What is likely to happen next?", using models and statistical techniques to forecast future outcomes. Prescriptive analytics answers "What should we do?" by recommending actions using optimisation or simulations. It focuses on decision-making, not identifying why something occurred.

3 The correct answers are:

	✓
Data must be collected for specified, explicit, and legitimate purposes.	✓
Personal data should be kept indefinitely so future needs can be met.	
Personal data must be accurate and kept up to date.	✓
Organisations should share personal data with any third party that requests it.	

Data must be collected for specified, explicit, and legitimate purposes is correct because it reflects the GDPR principle of purpose limitation, which requires organisations to clearly define why they are collecting personal data and ensures it is not reused for unrelated or inappropriate purposes. Similarly, personal data must be accurate and kept up to date is also correct, as it represents the GDPR accuracy principle. This principle requires organisations to maintain correct information and to correct or remove data that is inaccurate or outdated.

Personal data should be kept indefinitely so future needs can be met is incorrect because it conflicts with the GDPR storage limitation principle, which requires organisations to keep personal data only for as long as it is genuinely needed, and not retain it "just in case." Likewise, organisations should share personal data with any third party that requests it is incorrect because it violates the integrity and confidentiality principle. Data may only be shared when there is a lawful basis to do so, and organisations must protect personal data from unauthorised access or disclosure.

4 Phishing involves a cyberattacker sending emails to a victim which appear to be from a trusted source, for example a bank. The emails request the victim sends back security information (such as usernames and passwords) and personal details and uses them to steal funds from the victim.

5 The correct answer is:

	✓
Data is collected only from people who respond to an online survey, excluding those without internet access.	✓
The data analyst accidentally mistypes several values when entering results.	
A sensor records temperatures incorrectly because it is poorly calibrated.	
A model performs poorly because it was trained on high quality images but used on low quality images.	

Data is collected only from people who respond to an online survey, excluding those without internet access is correct because it represents sampling bias. Sampling bias occurs when the group selected for data collection is not representative of the entire population. In this case, only individuals with internet access and willingness to respond are included, meaning key groups are systematically excluded. As a result, the dataset is skewed and cannot accurately reflect the views or characteristics of the wider population.

The data analyst accidentally mistypes several values when entering results is not an example of sampling bias, but rather data entry error, which is a human mistake rather than a bias in how the sample was chosen. A sensor records temperatures incorrectly because it is poorly calibrated represents measurement bias, caused by flawed equipment producing consistently inaccurate readings. A model performs poorly because it was trained on high quality images but used on low quality images describes algorithmic bias or dataset mismatch, where the training data and real world data differ in quality or characteristics.

Chapter 5

1 The correct answer is:

	✓
Policies aimed at improving efficiency including reducing waste, using less energy and recycling	
A long-term programme involving a series of sustainable development practices aimed at improving organisational efficiency, stakeholder support and market edge	✓
A core part of an organisation's corporate social responsibility comprising efficiency, stakeholder support and market edge	

2 The six capitals are:

- Financial
- Manufactured
- Intellectual
- Human
- Social and relationship
- Natural

3 The correct answers are:

	✓
Climate-related topical risks	
Adverse climate-related opportunities	
Climate-related transition risks	✓
Chronic climate-related physical risks	✓
Acute climate-related changes	
Climate-related opportunities	✓

IFRS S2 considers climate-related risks and opportunities.

Climate-related risks can be categorised into physical and transition risks. The physical risks can be further divided into acute physical risks and chronic physical risks.

Climate-related topical risks, adverse climate-related opportunities and acute climate-related changes are not within the scope of IFRS S2.

4 The correct answer is:

	✓
IFRS Sustainability Disclosure Standards are issued by the IFRS Accounting Standards Board	
IFRS Sustainability Disclosure Standard have replaced the Integrated Reporting Framework	
There are currently 19 IFRS Sustainability Disclosure Standards in issue	
The sustainability disclosures required by the IFRS Sustainability Disclosure Standards are targeted at the primary users of general purpose financial reporting	✓

IFRS Sustainability Disclosure Standards are issued by the IFRS Sustainability Standards Board. These standards sit alongside the Integrated Reporting Framework, and have not replaced it. Currently, there are two IFRS Sustainability disclosures standards in issue – IFRS S1 and IFRS S2.

5 The correct answer is:

	✓
Greenwashing is when a company under communicates its sustainability efforts, while greenhushing is when it exaggerates them to appear more ecofriendly.	
Greenwashing is the act of deceptively overstating sustainability claims, whereas greenhushing is intentional silence or under communication about genuine sustainability actions.	✓
Greenwashing and greenhushing both refer to misleading claims about sustainability, but greenhushing involves providing too much technical detail.	
Greenwashing is always accidental, while greenhushing is always deliberate.	

Greenwashing involves companies exaggerating or misrepresenting their environmental practices to appear more sustainable than they are. Greenhushing, in contrast, refers to companies deliberately withholding or minimizing communication about their genuine sustainability progress, often out of fear of scrutiny or backlash. These definitions clearly distinguish one as over claiming and the other as under claiming.

Glossary

Chapter 1: Understanding business decision making

Cost benefit analysis: Analysis of the costs and benefits to an organisation of a potential business decision.

Intangible benefits: Other benefits of the decision, which are both difficult to identify and quantify. For example, an improved business reputation or better customer experience).

Intangible costs: Costs that cannot be quantified in financial terms (such as the cost of lost customers if a new system is not introduced). These costs are often difficult to identify and quantify.

Market positioning: How customers perceive a brand or product relative to other brands or products.

When positioning products and services, most organisations want to achieve a clear, unique and positive position, such as the cheapest supermarket or highest-quality vehicle manufacturer.

Key considerations include the following.

- Many products are, in fact, very similar, and the key issue is to create a distinction in the customer's mind.
- Few products occupy a market space on their own. Inevitably they will be positioned in relation to competing products.
- People remember 'number 1', so the product should be positioned as 'number 1' in relation to a positioning variable.

Mission: An expression of overall purpose and scope of the organisation in line with the values and expectations of stakeholders. It answers the question – what sort of business are we or do we want to be?

Objectives: Specific targets that set and control the overall functioning and progress of the organisation in order to meet its strategy.

Strategy: The organisation's plan of how to get from where it is now to where it wants to be in the future.

TQM: 'An integrated and comprehensive system of planning and controlling all business functions so that products or services are produced which meet or exceed customer expectations. TQM is a philosophy of business behaviour, embracing principles such as employee involvement, continuous improvement at all levels and customer focus [...]' (CIMA Official Terminology).

Tangible benefits: Benefits to the business of making the decision (such as improved efficiency) that are easy to identify. However, they may be hard to quantify precisely, and estimates or projections will be open to debate.

Tangible costs: Identified, quantifiable costs relating to a decision (such as the cost of new office equipment).

Vision: The desired future state of the organisation. Generally, this will be high level and timeless.

Chapter 2: Understanding organisational effectiveness

Collaboration: The process of working jointly with colleagues, departments, or stakeholders to achieve a shared objective. It involves combining skills, knowledge, and resources to produce outcomes that are better than what individuals could achieve alone.

Delegation: The process where one person (often a superior) gives another (often a subordinate) part of their own authority to make decisions or to perform a task.

Diversity: A concept which recognises and respects the fact that every individual is different and has their own unique characteristics.

Equity, diversity and inclusion (EDI) policies: A policy sets out an organisation's commitment to treating everyone fairly, valuing differences, and ensuring that all employees feel respected and able to contribute. It provides guidance on preventing discrimination, promoting equal opportunities, and creating a workplace culture where diverse perspectives are encouraged and supported.

Equity: An approach to the management of people at work based on equal access and fair treatment, irrespective of their background (for example, their gender, race, ethnicity, age, disability, sexual orientation and religious belief).

Escalation: The process of raising an issue, risk, or concern to a more senior person or appropriate authority when it cannot be resolved at the current level or within your responsibility.

Important tasks: Tasks that have major value or potential consequences for the organisation: for example, preparing an investment appraisal for a major project, or information needed for a board meeting.

Inclusion: The practice of creating a workplace where everyone feels respected, valued, and able to contribute fully, regardless of their background or personal characteristics. It's not just about having a diverse workforce (the mix of people) or ensuring fairness (equity); inclusion is about making sure every individual feels they belong and can participate meaningfully.

Reflective practice: The habit of taking time to look back on your actions, decisions, and outcomes to understand what went well, what could have been improved, and what you can do differently next time. It encourages individuals to pause, think, and learn from real experiences rather than simply moving from task to task on autopilot.

Routine tasks: Tasks which you perform almost daily and are most likely set out in your job description (for example, processing expenses, performing bank reconciliations or creating financial reports).

Unconscious bias: The automatic, unintentional attitudes, beliefs, or assumptions that influence decisions and behaviour without us being aware of them. These biases develop over time through our experiences, culture, and environment, and can affect how we perceive people or situations even when we aim to be fair and objective.

Unexpected tasks: Tasks that do not occur on a daily basis. For example, they may be one-off special jobs, such as covering for an employee who is on leave or assisting a colleague to meet an important deadline. Although unexpected, these tasks are still part of general working life, and you will need to fit them into your work schedule. To do this you will need to adjust your plans and priorities to take account of changing demands.

Urgent tasks: Tasks that must be completed for a deadline in the near future. For example, the Marketing Director may request a breakdown of sales by product for a meeting first thing tomorrow morning.

Chapter 3: Understanding ethics and law in an accounting environment

Ethical values: Assumptions and beliefs about what constitutes 'right' and 'wrong' behaviour.

Ethics: A set of moral principles that guide behaviour.

Money laundering: Attempts to make the proceeds of crime appear respectable. It covers any activity by which the apparent source and ownership of money representing the proceeds of income are changed so that the money appears to have been obtained legitimately.

Whistleblowing: is the name commonly given to workers making a disclosure of wrongdoing (usually) by their employer.

Chapter 4: Understanding the effective use of data in business

Accurate information: Information that is factually and numerically correct. In other words, the information is supported by evidence and all the numbers and any calculations work mathematically.

Artificial intelligence (AI): The development of computer systems that can perform tasks normally requiring human intelligence. These tasks include recognising patterns, learning from data, making decisions and solving problems. In business, AI supports automation, analysis, forecasting and improved decision making.

Causation: When one variable directly influences or produces a change in another.

Correlation: A relationship or association between two variables – when one changes, the other also tends to change.

Cyber-risk: A term that covers a number of organisational risks which are possible consequences of a cyberattack. Cyber-risks include financial losses, reputational damage and operational disruption.

Cyberattacks: Deliberate attempts to damage an organisation by using the Internet to take advantage of poor security controls and system integrity.

Cybersecurity: The protection of computer systems from the risk of cyberattack through the use of hardware and software security procedures and controls.

Data analytics: The collection, management and analysis of large data sets with the objective of discovering useful information that an organisation can use for decision making.

Data bias: Data bias occurs when the information collected, analysed or presented does not accurately represent the real situation, leading to misleading or unfair conclusions. Bias can arise unintentionally through poor data collection, incorrect sampling, flawed assumptions or human judgement.

Data cleansing: The process of identifying and correcting errors, gaps and inconsistencies within a dataset to ensure that the information a business uses is accurate, complete, reliable and fit for analysis.

Data visualisation: The presentation of data in a pictorial or graphical format which is easier for recipients to process than detailed written data.

Invalid information: The direct opposite of valid information. It is not relevant or strongly associated with the purpose it is being put to and therefore it is not appropriate to use it.

Negligent errors: Negligent errors arise from carelessness or failure to follow proper procedures during data entry, collection, or processing.

Primary information: Information collected specifically for a particular purpose.

Random errors: Random errors are unexpected, unpredictable variations in data that occur without a consistent pattern. They often result from temporary conditions or human variation.

Reliable information: Information that can be trusted, depended upon and can be considered genuine and authentic.

Sampling: Sampling involves collecting data from a smaller, representative subset of the full population. The results are then used to estimate or predict what is likely to be true for the whole group.

Secondary information: Information collected for some other purpose than what it is being used for.

Systematic errors: Systematic errors occur when data is consistently incorrect in the same direction or pattern. They stem from flaws in the data collection process, measuring tools, or procedures.

Valid information: Information that is relevant, strongly associated, and appropriate to the purpose it is being used for.

Whole population data: Also called a census, **whole population data collection** involves collecting information from every individual, item or event within the group being studied.

Chapter 5: Understanding the importance of sustainability in business

Acute climate-related physical risks : Event-drive climate-related risks relating to weather-related events such as storms, floods, drought or heatwaves.

Capitals: The broad categories of resources and relationships that an organisation uses or affects in creating value over time. They represent the different "stocks" of value – financial and non financial – that the organisation draws on as inputs to its business model and that are increased, decreased, or transformed through its activities and outputs. The capitals provide a holistic way of understanding how value is created, preserved, or eroded beyond financial performance alone.

Chronic climate-related physical risks : Longer-term shifts in climatic patterns including changes in precipitation and temperature which have an impact on the environment eg reduced water availability, biodiversity loss

Climate-related opportunities : The potential positive effects arising from climate change for an entity.

IFRS S2 Appendix A

Climate-related physical risks : Risks arising from climate-related events or changes e.g. hurricanes or rising sea temperatures

Climate-related transition risks : Policy, legal, technological, market and reputational risks that arise from the transition to a lower-carbon economy

Sustainability: According to the **UN's Brundtland Report** (World Commission on Environment and Development, 1987) **sustainability** means that organisations must aim to 'meet the needs of the present without compromising the ability of future generations to meet their own needs'.

Value chain: The full range of interactions, resources and relationships related to a reporting entity's business model and the external environment in which operates. (IFRS S1, Appendix A)

Bibliography

Adair, J. (2009) Effective Time Management, Basingstoke: Pan Macmillan.

Association of Accounting Technicians (2017) AAT Code of Professional Ethics [Online]. Available at: https://www.aat.org.uk/prod/s3fs-public/assets/AAT-Code-Professional-Ethics.pdf [Accessed 28 March 2026].

Bribery Act 2010 (2010) [Online]. Available from: www.legislation.gov.uk [Accessed 28 March 2026]

CIMA (2005) *CIMA Official Terminology*. Oxford, CIMA

CIMA (2020) *Managing finance in a digital world*. Wokingham: Kaplan Publishing.

Covey, Stephen R. (1990) *The 7 Habits of Highly Effective People*, Simon & Schuster.

Data Protection Act 2018. (2018) [Online]. Available from: www.legislation.gov.uk [Accessed 30 March 2026].

Ellen MacArthur Foundation (no date) *What is the meaning of a circular economy and what are the main principles?* [online] Available from: https://www.ellenmacarthurfoundation.org/topics/circular-economy-introduction/overview [accessed 31 March 2026]

ISSB (no date) *International Sustainability Standards Board* [online] Available from: https://www.ifrs.org/groups/international-sustainability-standards-board/ [accessed 31 March 2026]

International Integrated Reporting Council (no date) *The IIRC* [online] Available from: http://integratedreporting.org/the-iirc-2/ [accessed 31 March 2026]

Kaplan, R. S. and Norton, D. P. (1996) *The Balanced Scorecard: Translating Strategy into Action*. Boston, Harvard Business School Press

Koontz, H. and O'Donnell, C. (1976) *Management: A Systems and Contingency Analysis of Managerial functions*. 6th Edition; New York: McGraw Hill Publisher.

Porter, M. (1980) *Competitive Strategy*. New York, Free Press.

Proceeds of Crime Act 2002 (2002) [Online]. Available from: www.legislation.gov.uk/ [Accessed 28 March 2026]

Public Interest Disclosure Act 1998 (1998) [Online]. Available from: www.legislation.gov.uk/ [Accessed 28 March 2026]

Tufte, E.R. (2001) *The Visual Display of Quantitative Information*. 2nd Edition. Cheshire, CT, United States of America, Graphics Press.

UN (no date) *The 17 Goals* [online] Available from: https://sdgs.un.org/goals [accessed 31 March 2026]

World Commission on Environment and Development (1987) Our Common Future, New York: Oxford University Press.

Index

3

3 Ps, 125

A

AAT's Code of Professional Ethics, 64
Access, 97
Access control, 100
Accountability, 69
Accuracy, 97
Accurate information, 87
Action plans, 35
Ad clicker, 100
Advocacy, 67
Algorithmic Bias, 112
Artificial intelligence (AI), 104
Authorised disclosure, 72
Automated checks for duplicates, 93
Automated decision making and profiling, 98

B

Balanced scorecard, 9
Being bribed, 73
Bluewashing, 135
Boundary firewalls, 100
Bribery offences, 73
Bribing a foreign public official, 74
Bribing another person, 73
Brownspinning, 135
Business ethics, 62
Business letter, 39
Business reports, 40

C

Capitals, 121
Causation, 112
Circular economy, 123
Collaboration, 41, 42
Commercially sensitive information, 102
Communication, 37
Comparing data to known, reliable sources, 93
Comparison checks, 93
Competition, 17
Completeness checks, 93
Confidentiality, 64, 65
Confirmation Bias, 112
Conflict of interest, 65
Consequences of unethical behaviour, 69
Continuous improvement, 14
Corporate failure to prevent bribery, 74
Correlation, 112
Cost benefit analysis, 24
Cost leadership, 12
Cost-push inflation, 18
Courtesy, 68
Critical success factors (CSFs), 7
Cyber-risk, 99
Cyberattacks, 99
Cybersecurity, 99

D

Data analytics, 94
Data bias, 111
Data minimisation, 97
Data portability, 98
Data protection principles, 96
Data visualisation, 106
Degrowth, 123
Delegation, 41, 43
Demand pull inflation, 18
Descriptive analytics, 95
Diagnostic analytics, 96
Differentiation, 12
Digital applications,, 111
Discrimination, 45
Distributed denial of service (DDoS) attack, 100
Diversity, 46
Due care, 65
Duplication errors, 92

E

Economic factors affecting strategy and performance, 17
Economic growth, 17, 123
Effective communication, 38
Eisenhower Decision Matrix, 35
Email, 39
Employee resource groups, 47
Equity, 45
Equity, diversity and inclusion (EDI), 45

Equity, diversity and inclusion (EDI) policies, 48
Erasure, 97
Escalation, 41, 42
Ethical values, 60
Ethics, 60
Ethics (or Compliance) Officers, 62
Exchange rates., 18
External information, 88

F

Failure to report, 71
Familiarity, 67
File hijacker/ransomware, 100
Financial KPIs, 7
Fiscal policy, 17
Five fundamental ethical principles, 64
Focus, 12, 35

G

General Data Protection Regulation, 96
Goals, 35
Government policy, 17
Grants, 17
Greencrowding, 135
Greenflation, 135
Greenhushing, 135
Greenlighting, 135
Greenwashing, 135

H

Hacking, 99
Historical Bias, 112

I

IFRS S1 General Requirements for Disclosure of Sustainability-related Financial Information, 129
IFRS S2 Climate-related Disclosures, 130
Important tasks, 35
Inclusion, 46
Independenceof appearance, 68
Independence of mind, 68
Inflation, 18
Intangible benefits, 24
Intangible costs, 24
Integrated Reporting Framework, 121
Integration, 71
Integrity, 64, 64
Integrity and confidentiality, 97
Interest rates, 18
Internal information, 88
International Sustainability Standards Board (ISSB), 128
International trade, 18
International trade policy, 19
Internet gateways, 100
Intimidation, 67
Intranets, 41
Invalid information, 87

K

Key performance indicators (KPIs), 7
Keylogging, 100
Koontz and O'Donnell (1976), 44

L

Laundering, 71
Lawfulness, fairness and transparency, 96
Layering, 71

M

Macro-economics, 16
Malware, 100
Malware protection, 100
Market positioning, 11
Measurement Bias, 112
Measurement errors, 92
Meetings, 40
Messaging, 41
Mission, 4
Mission statements, 5
Monetary policy, 18

N

Narrative, 107
Negligent errors, 91
Non-financial KPIs, 7

O

Objectives, 4, 6
Objectivity, 64, 65

Operational objectives, 6
Organisation, 35
Organisation-wide philosophy, 14
Outlier and anomaly errors, 92

P

Patch management, 100
People, 125
Personal qualities, 68
PESTLE analysis, 21
Pharming, 99
Phishing, 99
Pillars of sustainability, 125
Placement, 71
Planet, 125
Planning your time, 34
Porter's potential positioning strategies, 11
Predictive analytics, 96
Prescriptive analytics, 96
Primary information, 86
Principles of TQM, 13
Priorities, 35
Prioritising, 35
Prioritising plans, 35
Procedures to prevent and detect money laundering, 73
Processing errors, 92
Professional behaviour, 64, 66
Professional competence, 65
Professional competence and due care, 64
Professional qualities, 68
Professional scepticism, 69
Profit, 125
Protected disclosure, 72, 74
Public Interest Disclosure Act 1998, 74
Purpose limitation, 97

R

Random errors, 91
Random sampling, 90
Recording data, 86
Rectification, 97
Reflective practice, 44
Registering for anti-money laundering supervision (AML), 72
Reliability, 68
Reliable information, 87
Reporting money laundering, 72
Respect, 68
Response Bias, 112
Responsibility, 68
Restrict processing, 97
Reviewing outliers or unusual patterns, 93
Right first time, 13
Routine tasks, 35

S

Sampling, 90
Sampling Bias, 111
Screenshot manager, 100
Secondary information, 86
Secure configuration, 101
Selection Bias, 112
Self-interest, 66
Self-review, 67
SMART, 6
Social media, 40, 109
Social responsibility, 69
Spreadsheet, 108
Spreadsheets, 40
Storage limitation, 97
Storage of data, 101
Strategic (corporate) objectives, 6
Strategy, 4
Stratified sampling, 90
Supply and demand, 19
Suspicious Activity Report, 72
Sustainability, 120
Sustainability challenges, 124
Sustainability policies and benefits of sustainability, 134
SWOT analysis, 23
System sampling, 90
Systematic errors, 91

T

Tactical objectives, 6
Tangible benefits, 24
Tangible costs, 24
The AAT Code of Professional Ethics, 64

Three pillars of sustainability , 125
Timeliness, 68
Tipping off, 71
To be informed, 97
To object, 98
Total Quality Management (TQM), 13
TQM, 13
Transcription errors, 92
Triple bottom line , 125
Trojan, 100

U

UN Sustainable Development Goals (UN SDGs), 126
Unconscious bias, 49
Unemployment, 19
Unexpected tasks, 35
Urgency, 35
Urgent tasks, 35

V

Valid information, 87
Validation rules, 93
Validation rules , 93
Virus protection, 100
Vision, 4
Vision statement, 4

W

Webcam manager, 100
Whistleblowing, 74
Whole population data, 89

Tell us what you think

Got comments or feedback on this book? Let us know.
Use your QR code reader:

Or, visit:
https://www.smartsurvey.co.uk/s/W30E6Y/

Need to get in touch with customer service?

www.bpp.com/request-support

Spotted an error?

https://learningmedia.bpp.com/pages/errata